I0436353

Tattoo Designs Coloring Book

✓ **50** Coloring pages 🖍

✓ Illustrations **for drawing or** tattoo **templates** 🎨

✓ **Ideal for** crayons, markers, **or colored** pencils ✏️

✓ Large print **page format:** 8.5 x 11 inches 📖

✓ Single-sided **pages to avoid bleed-through,** ensuring your masterpieces remain pristine 🖌

✓ Calming **and** relaxing **activity to explore** creativity 🖤

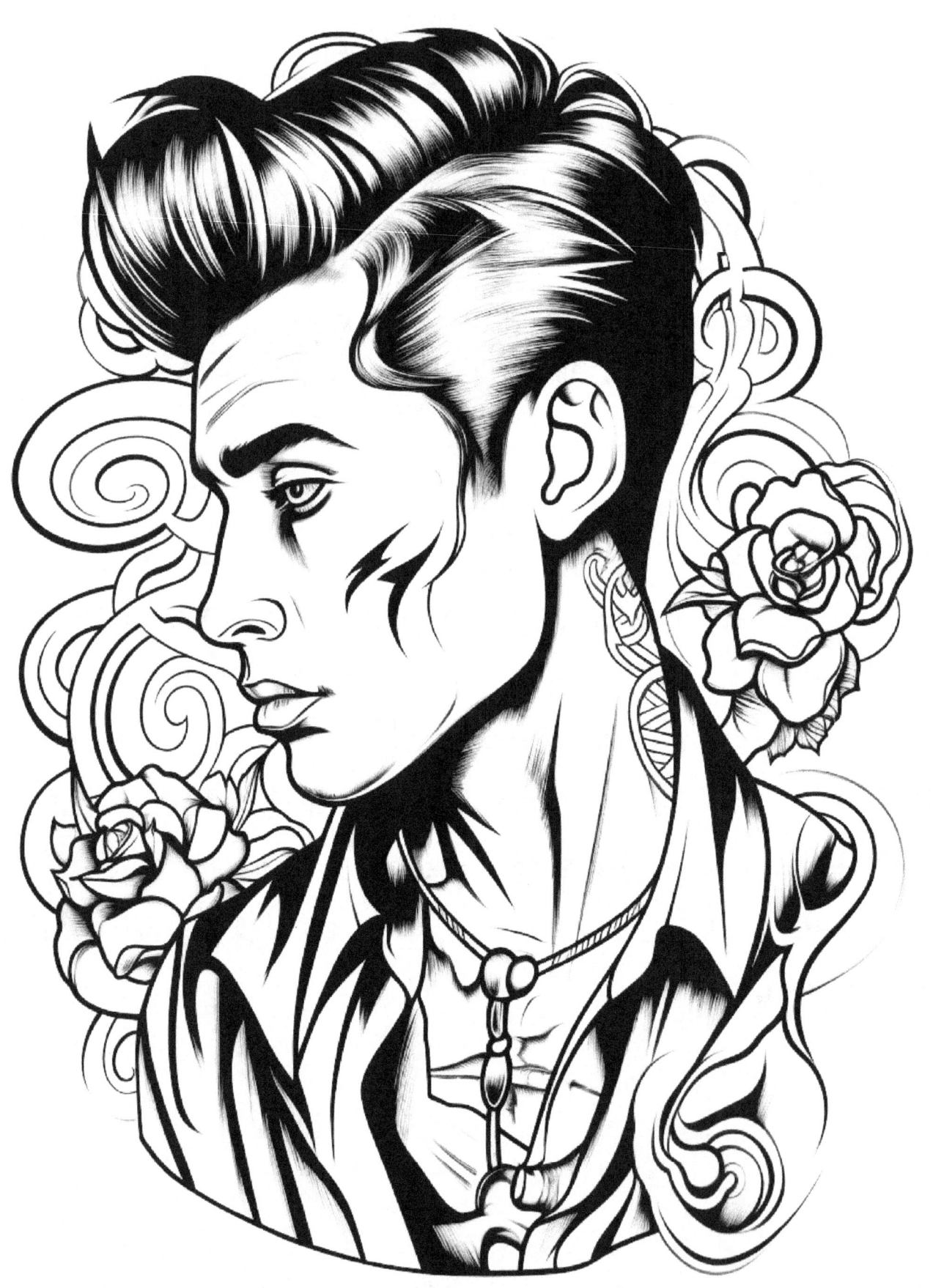

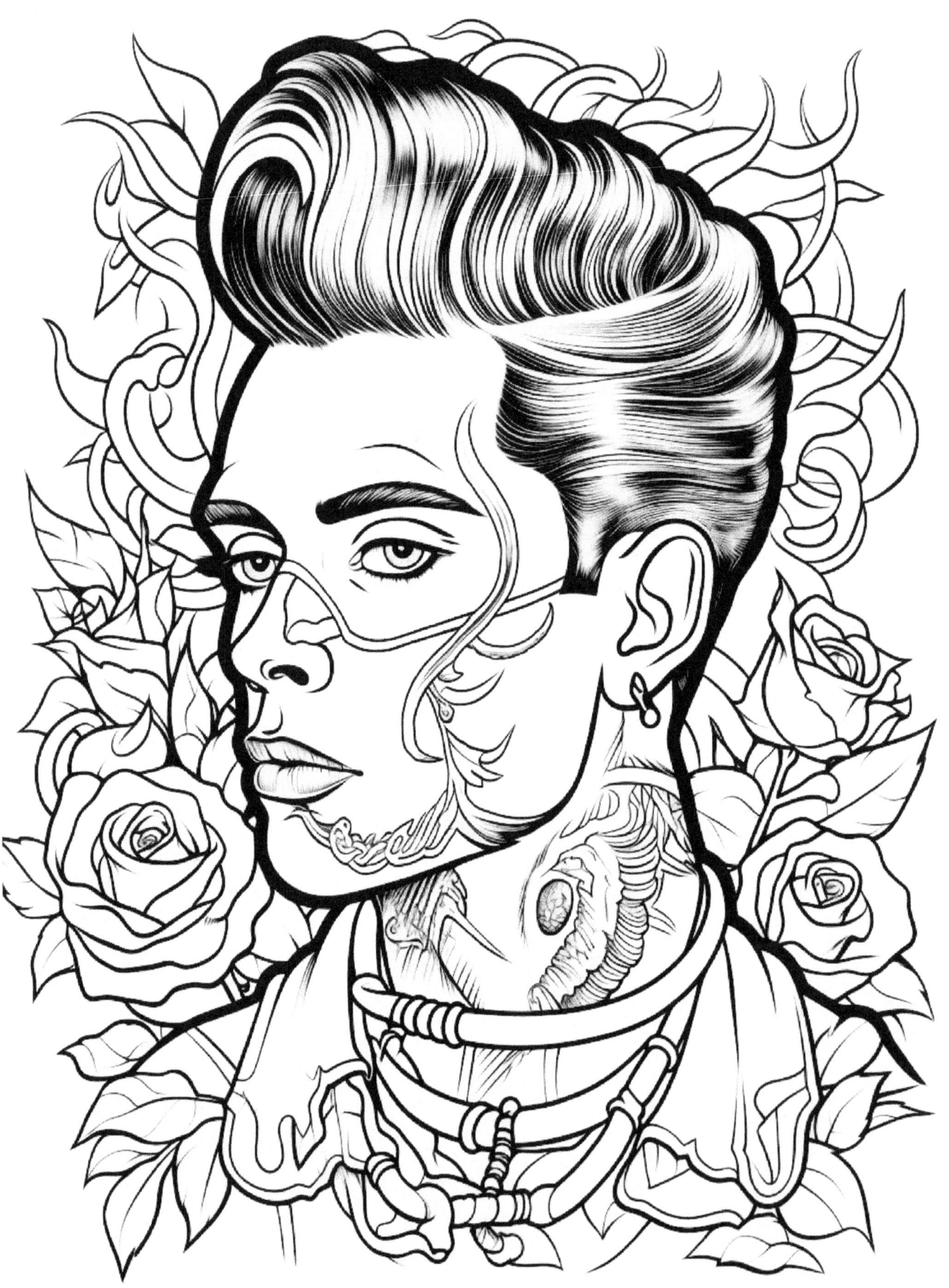

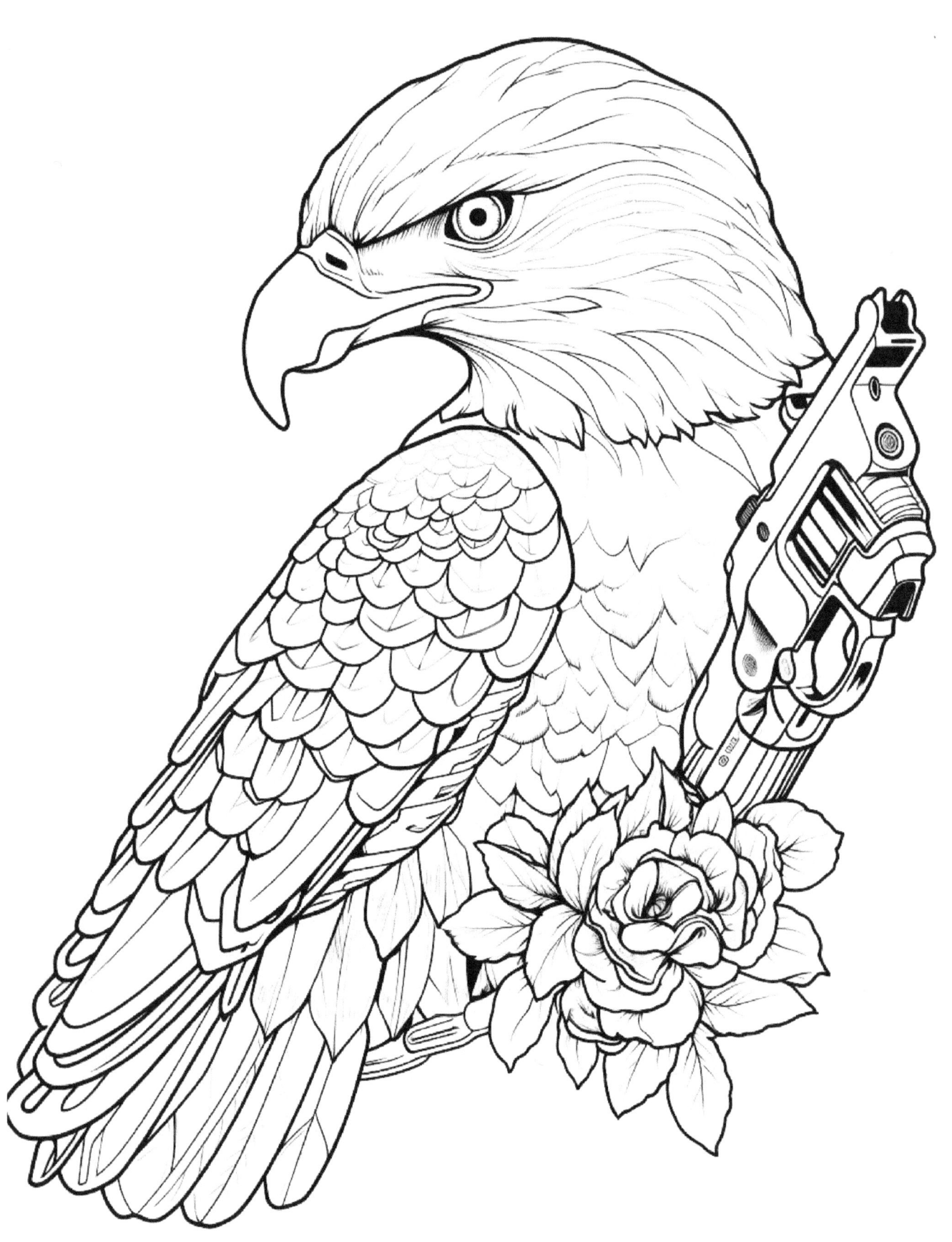

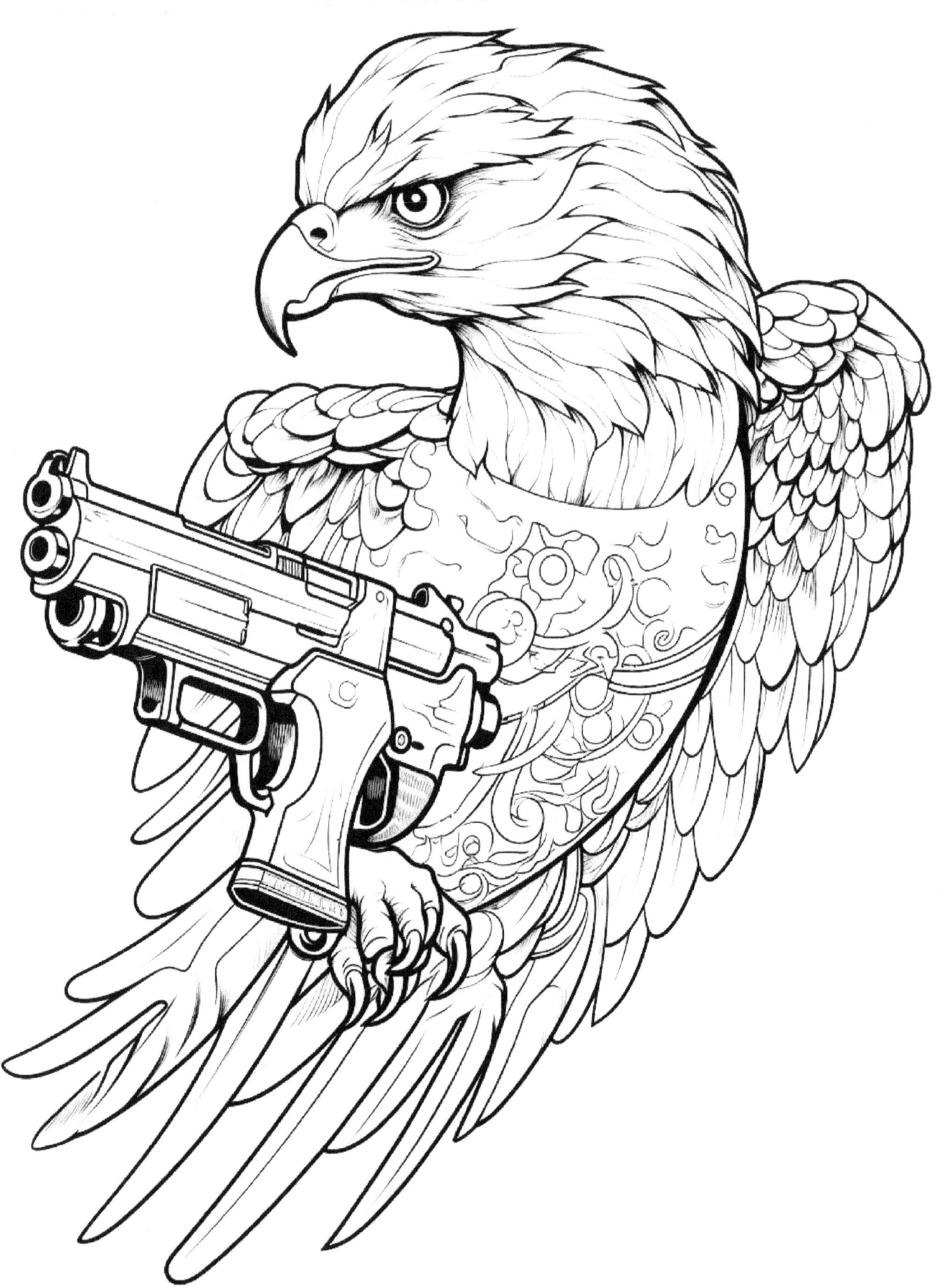

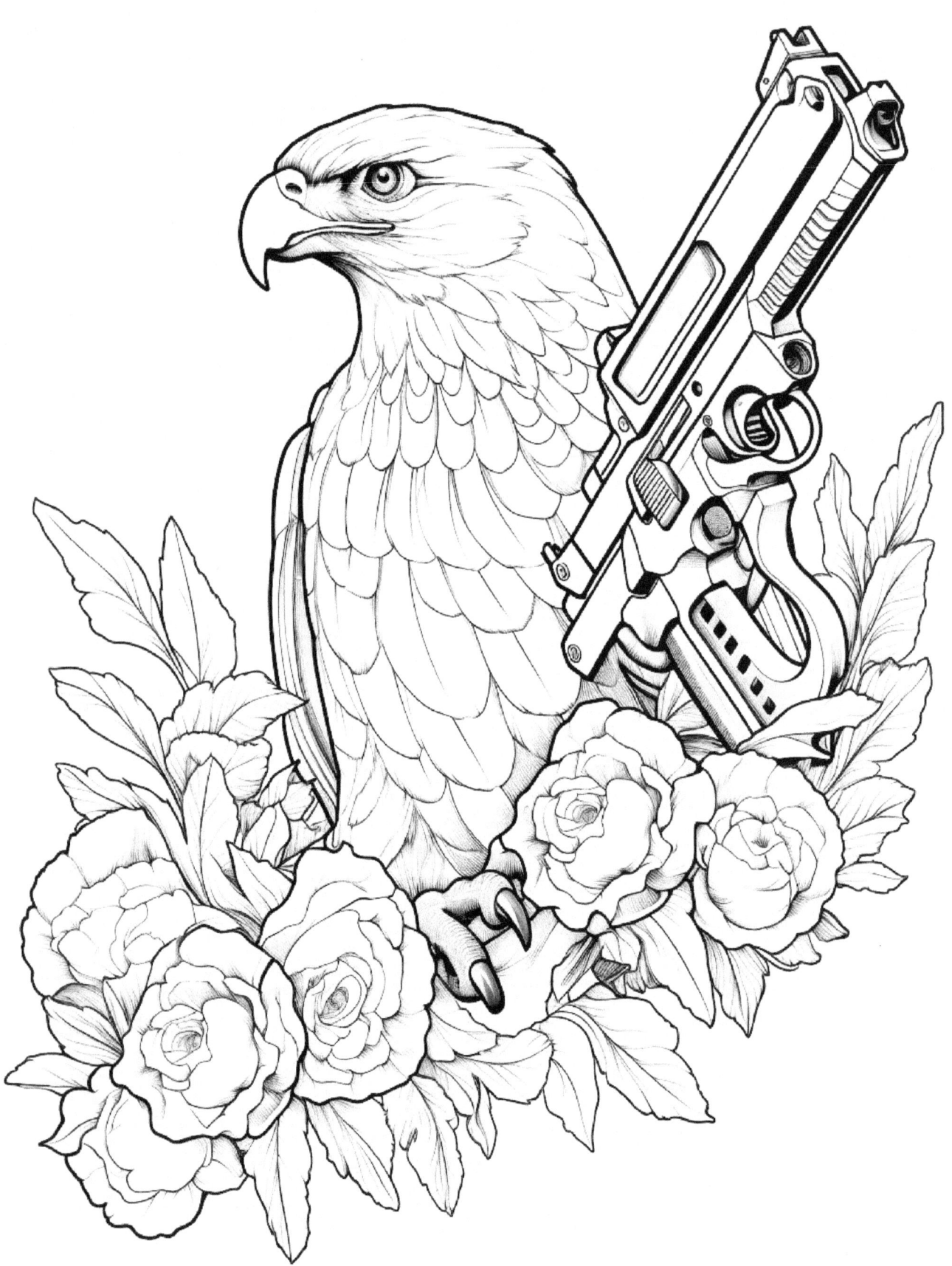

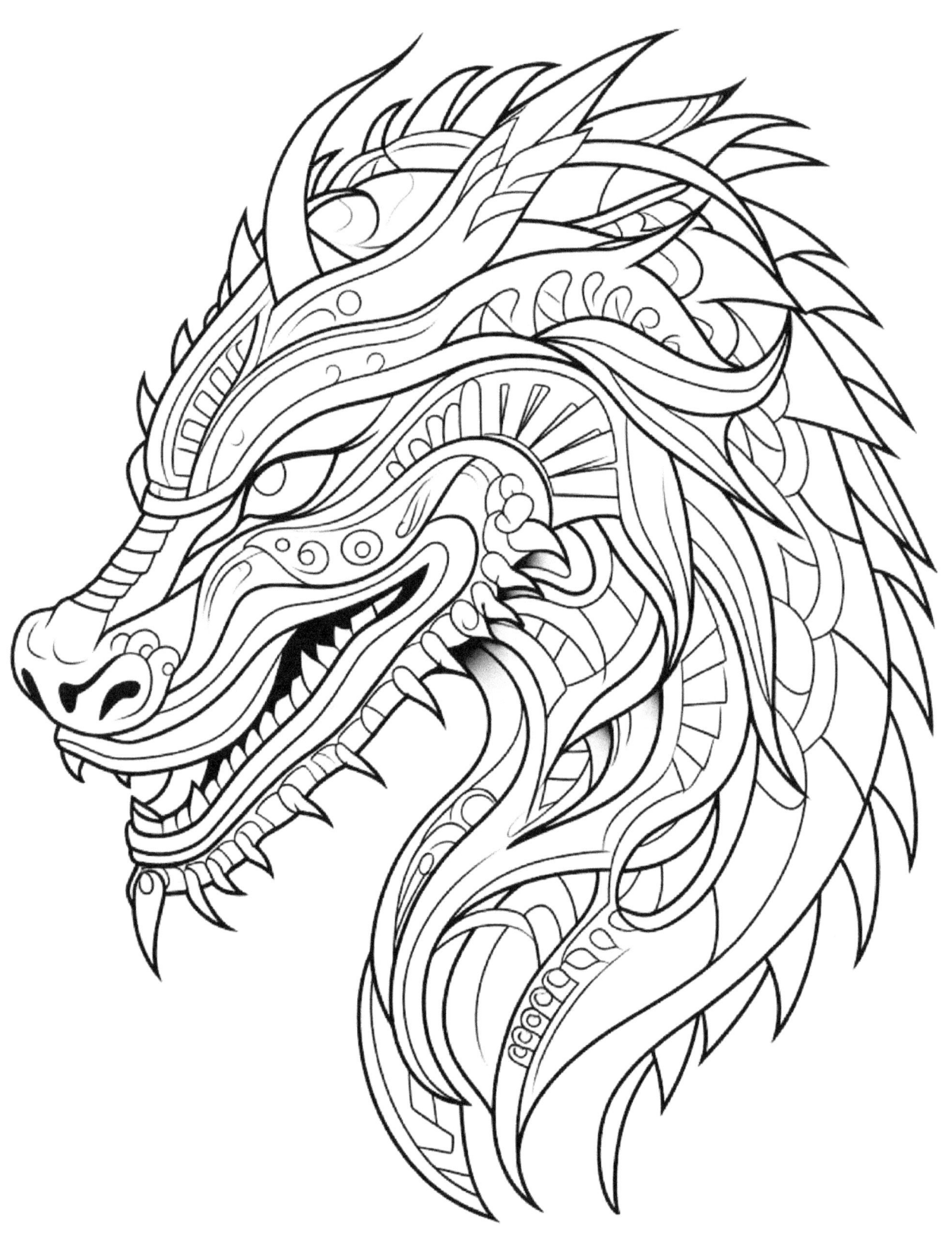

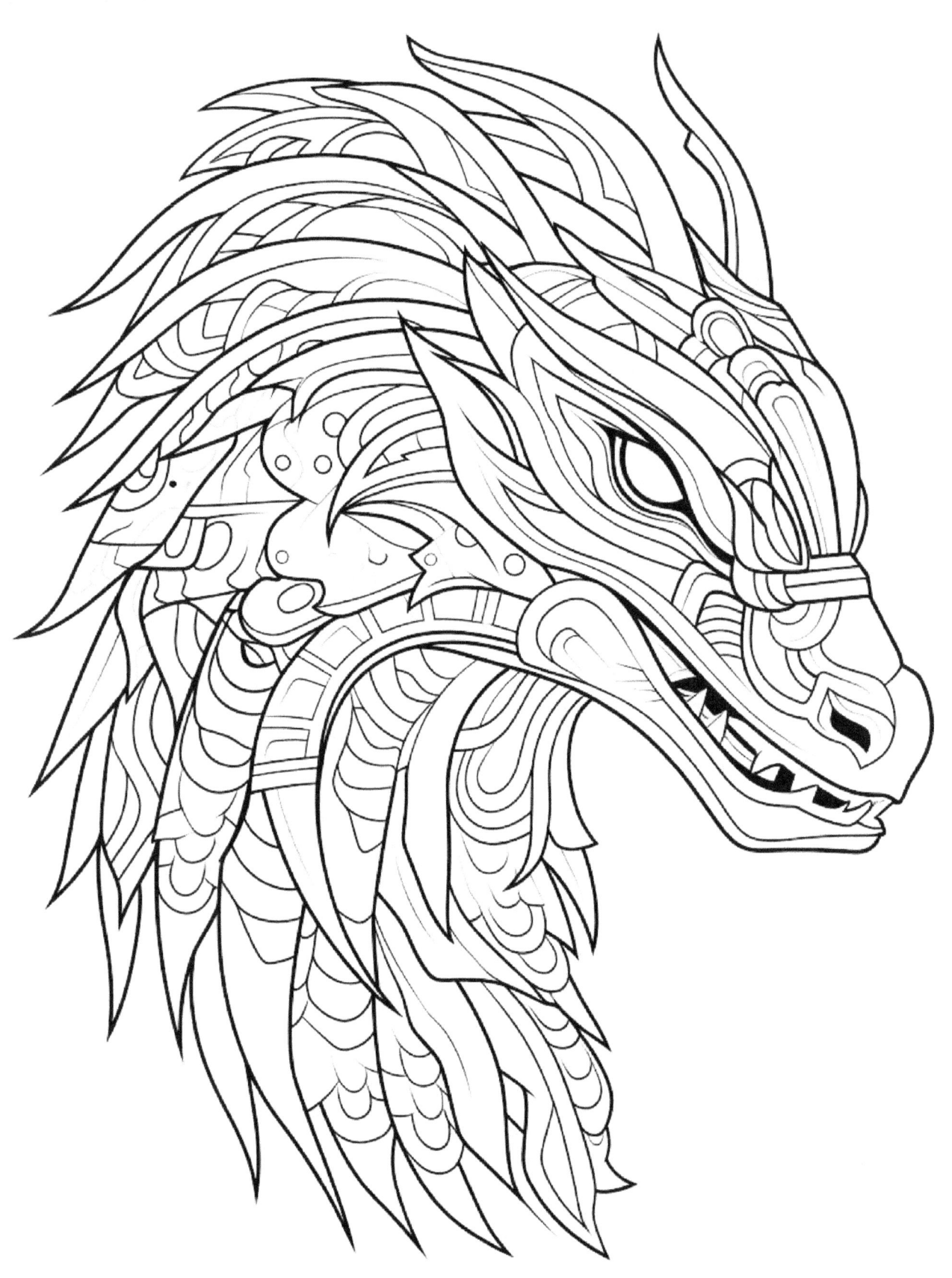

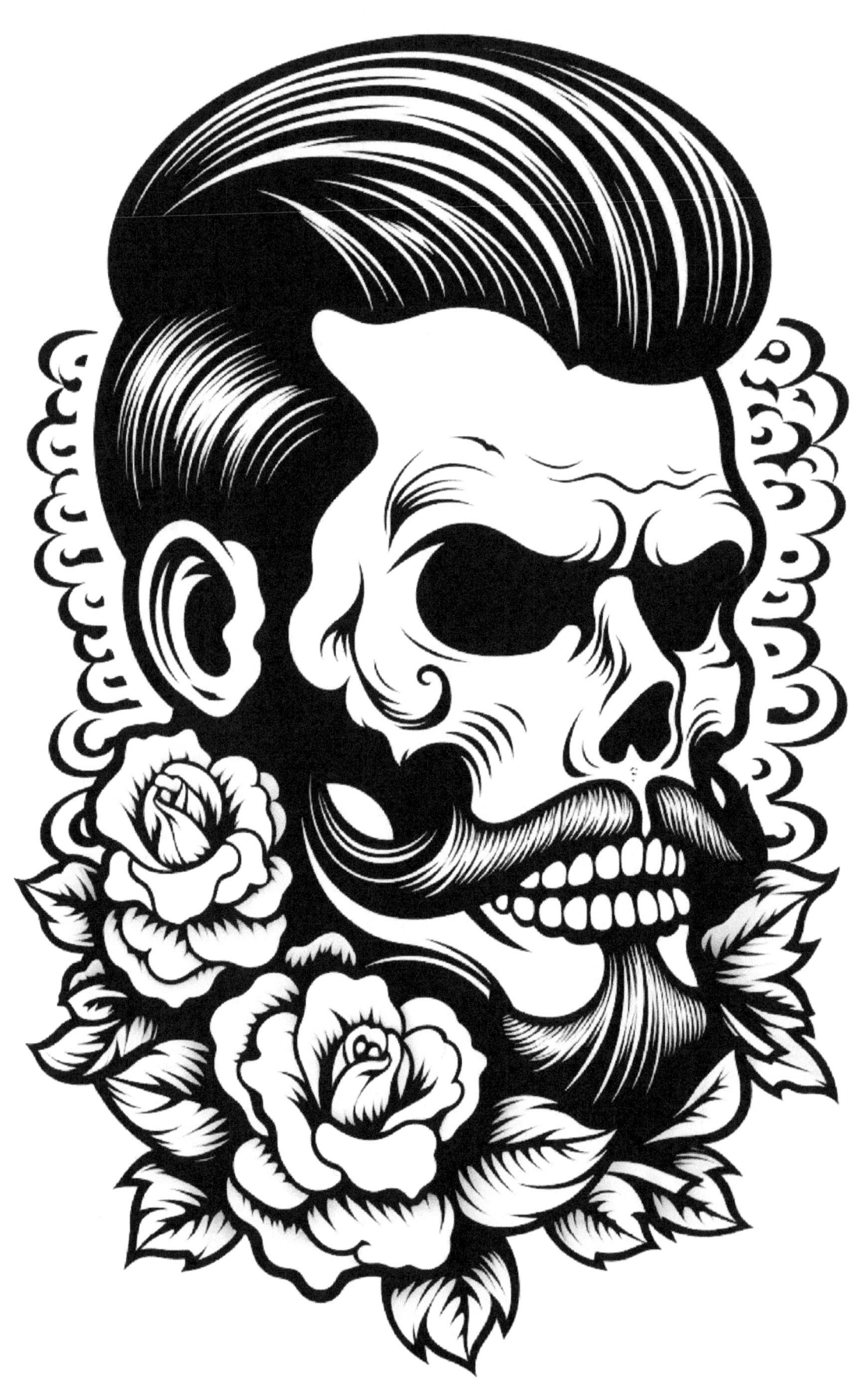

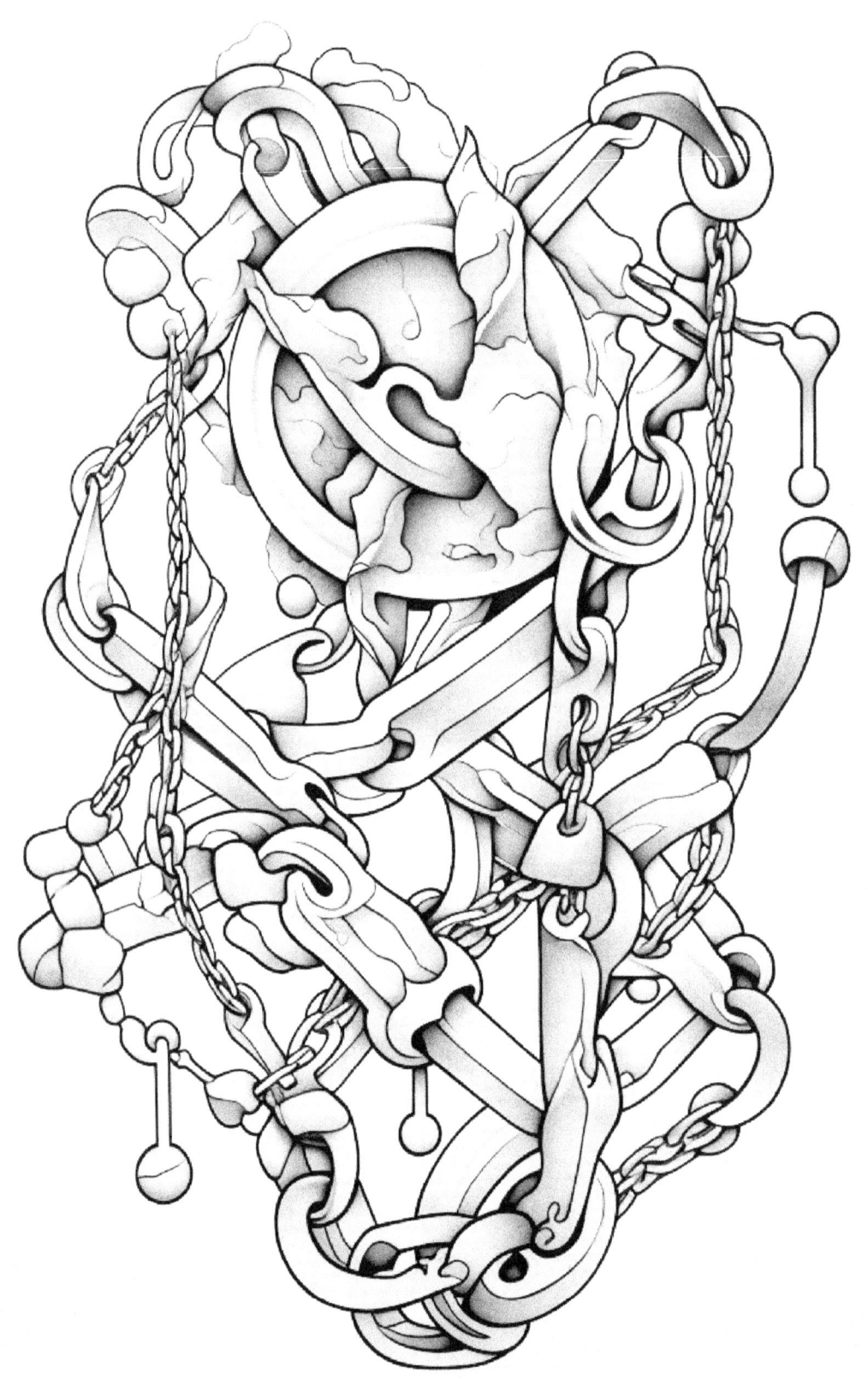

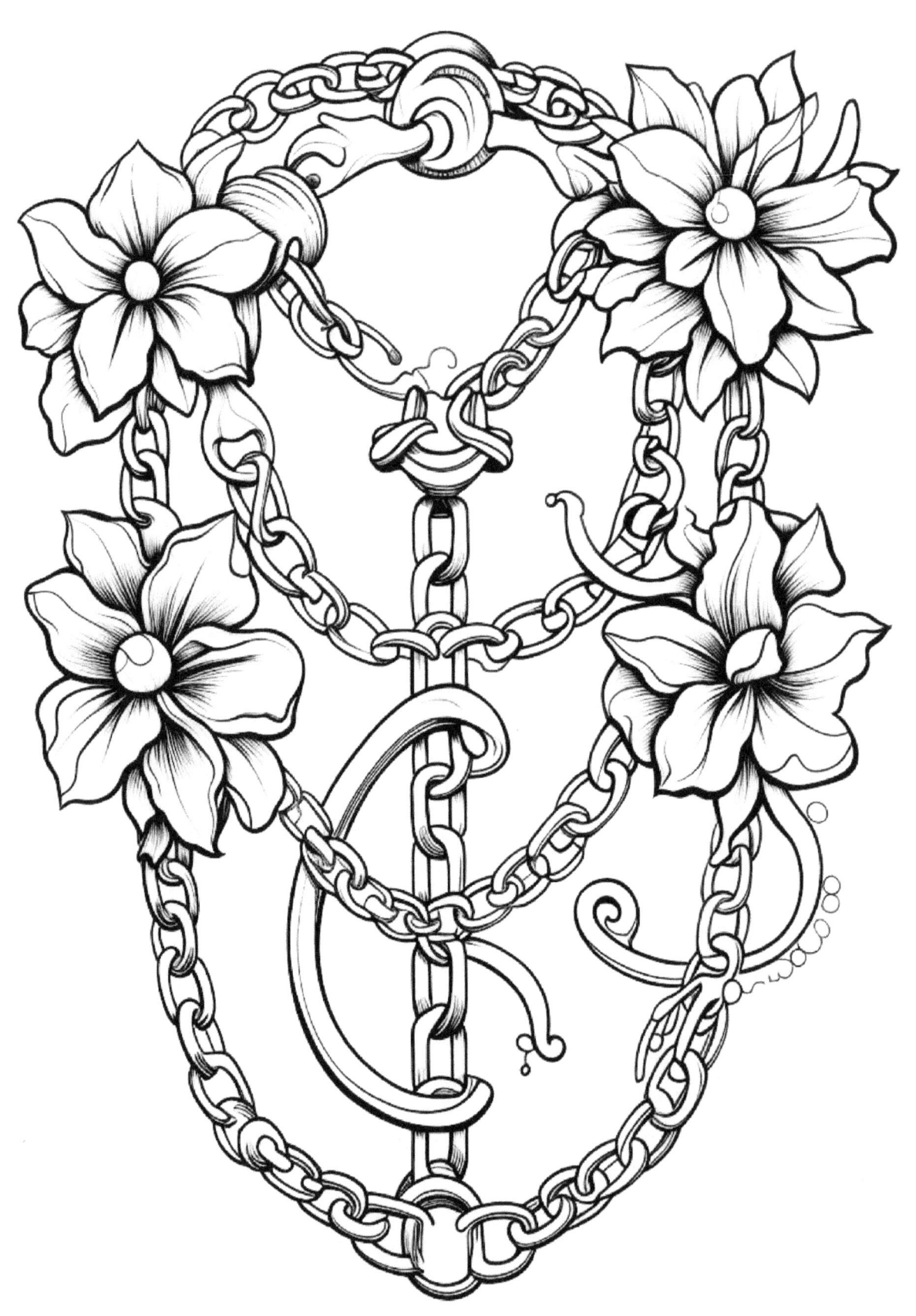

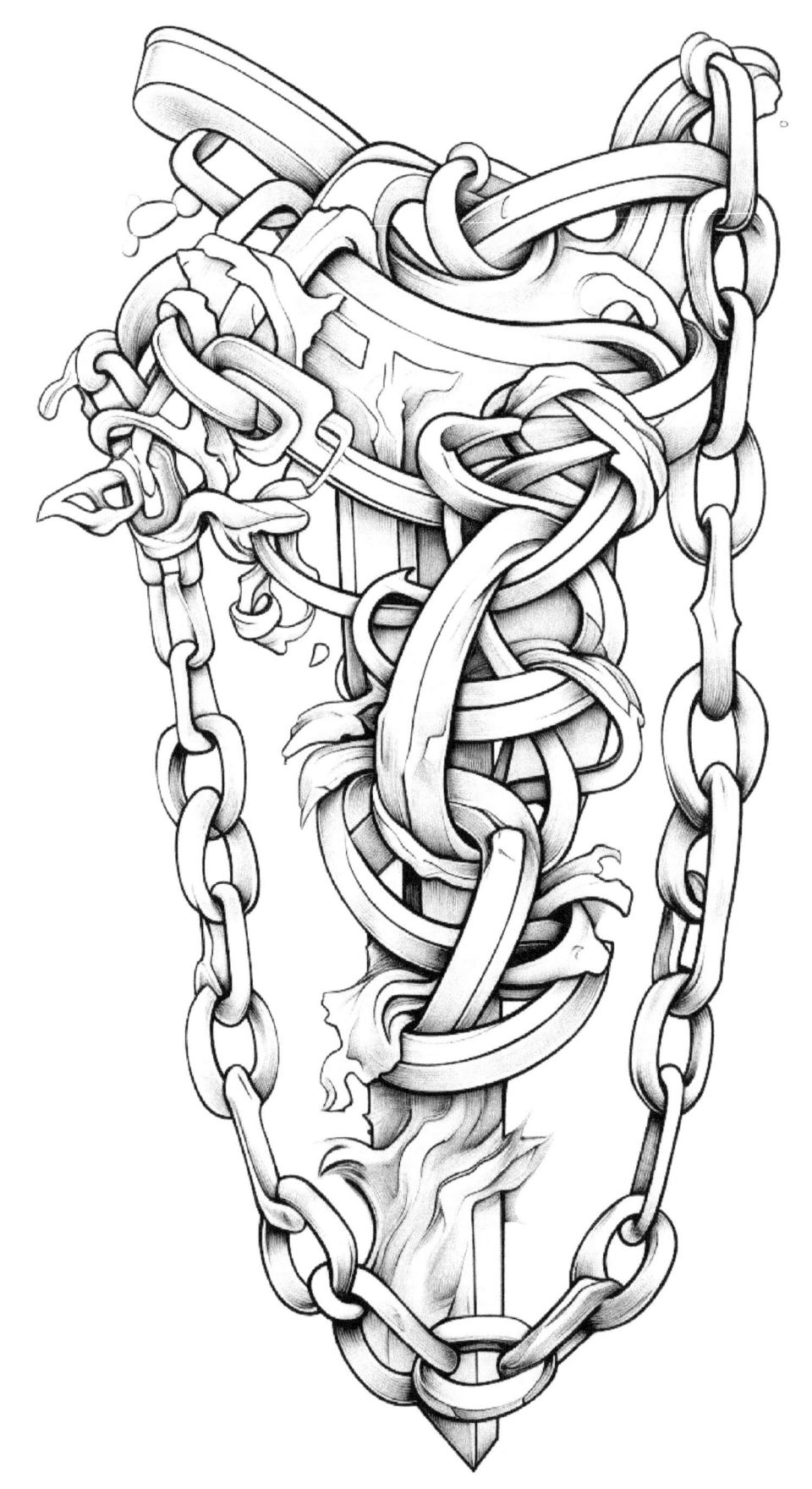

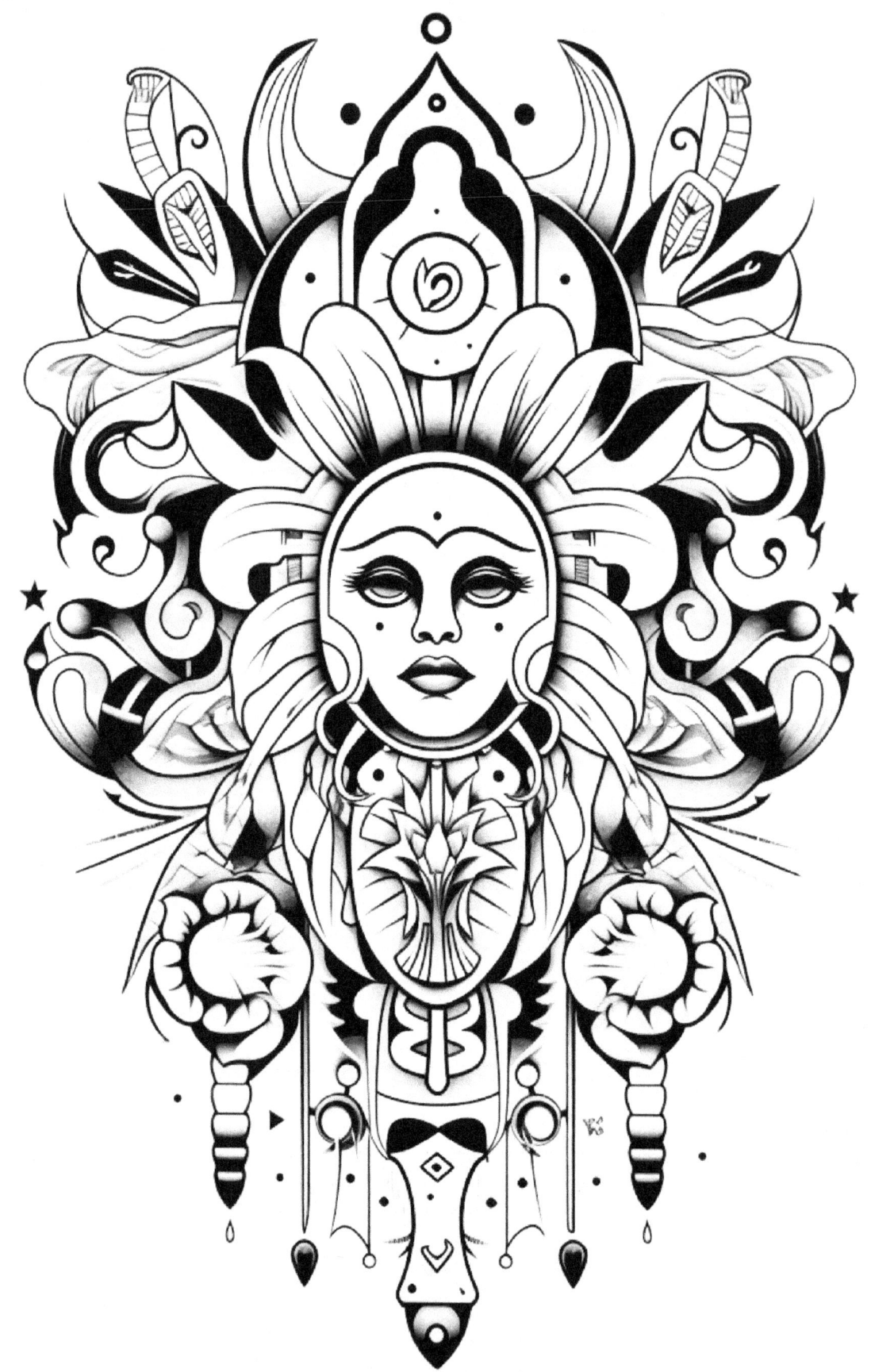

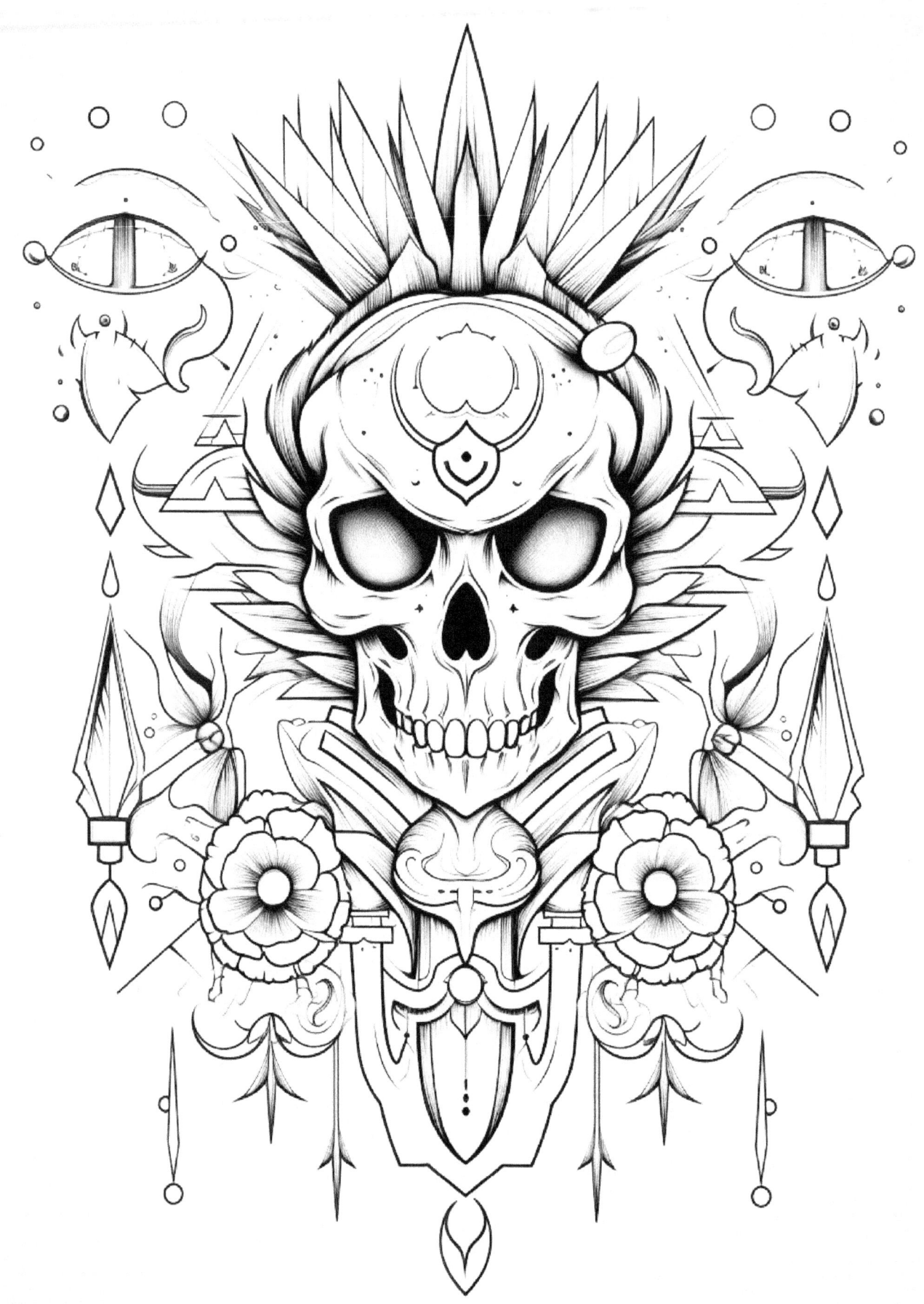

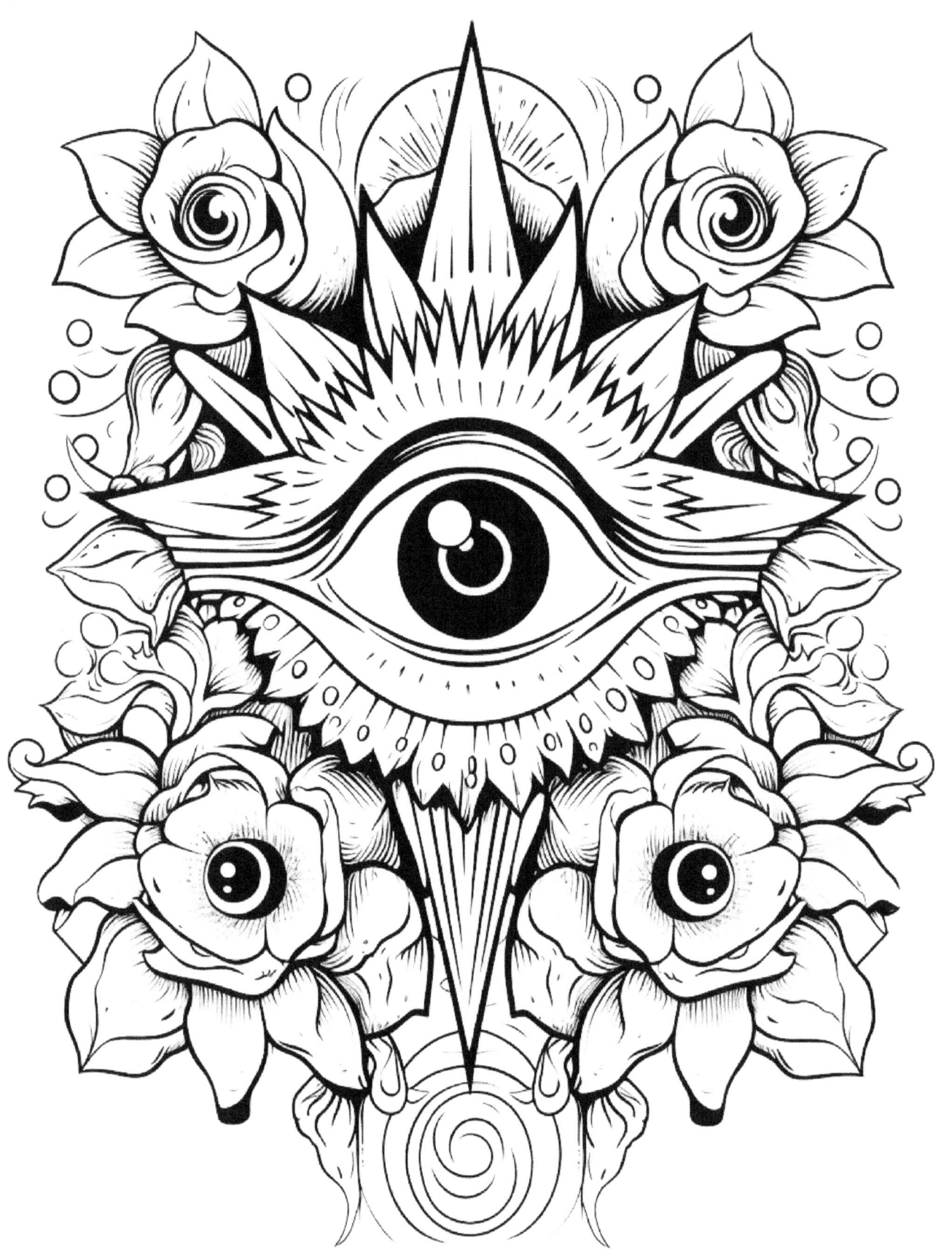

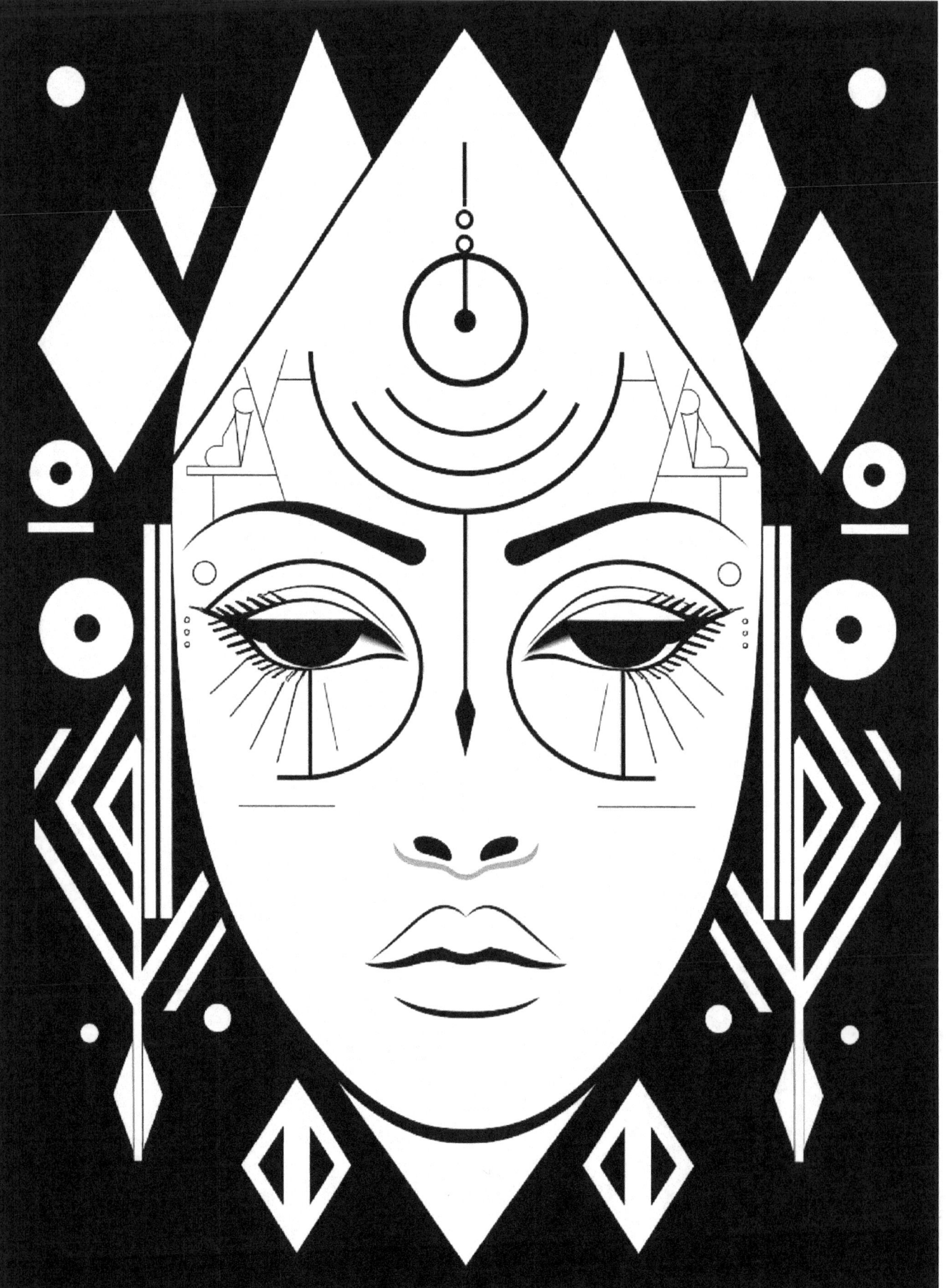

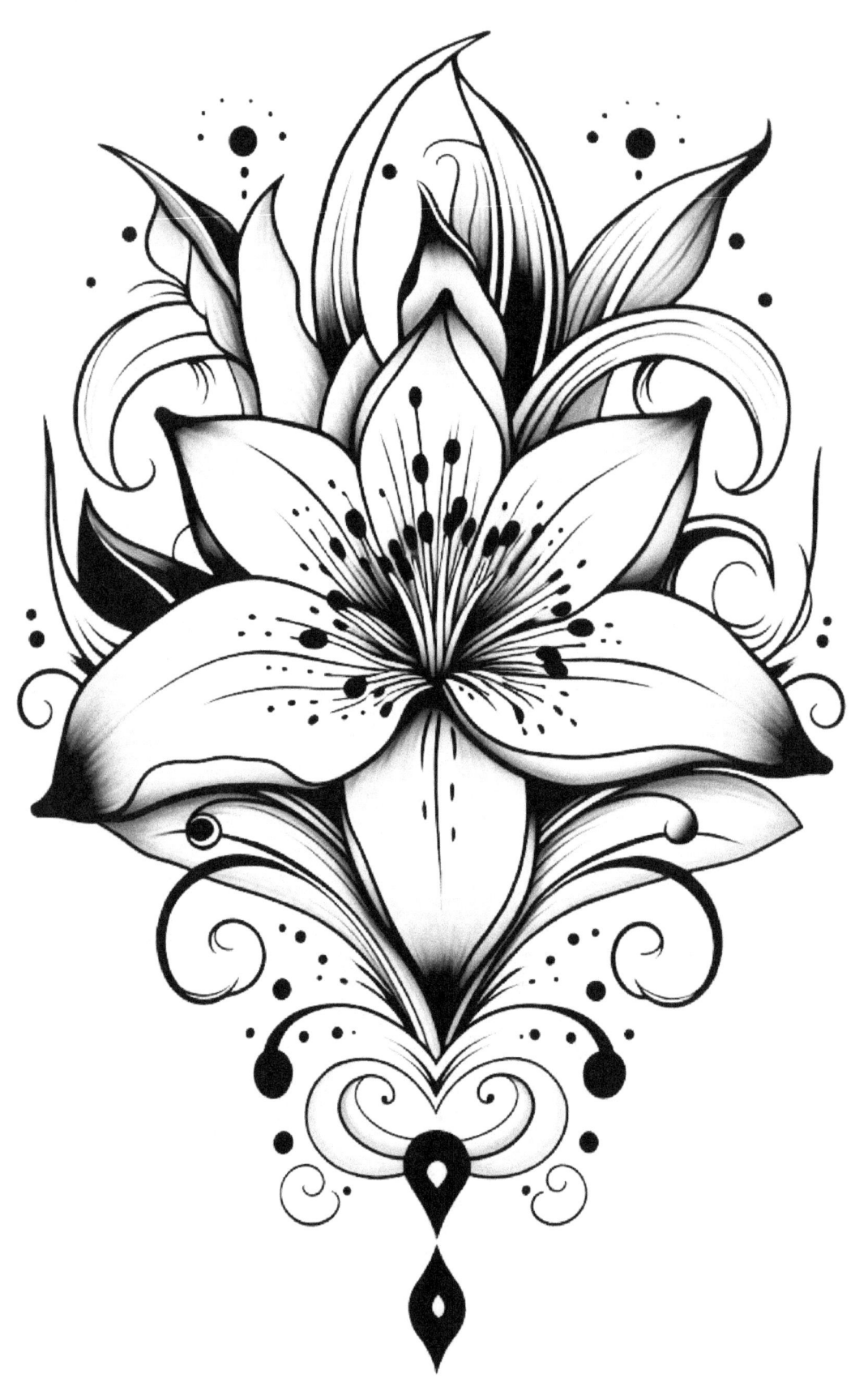

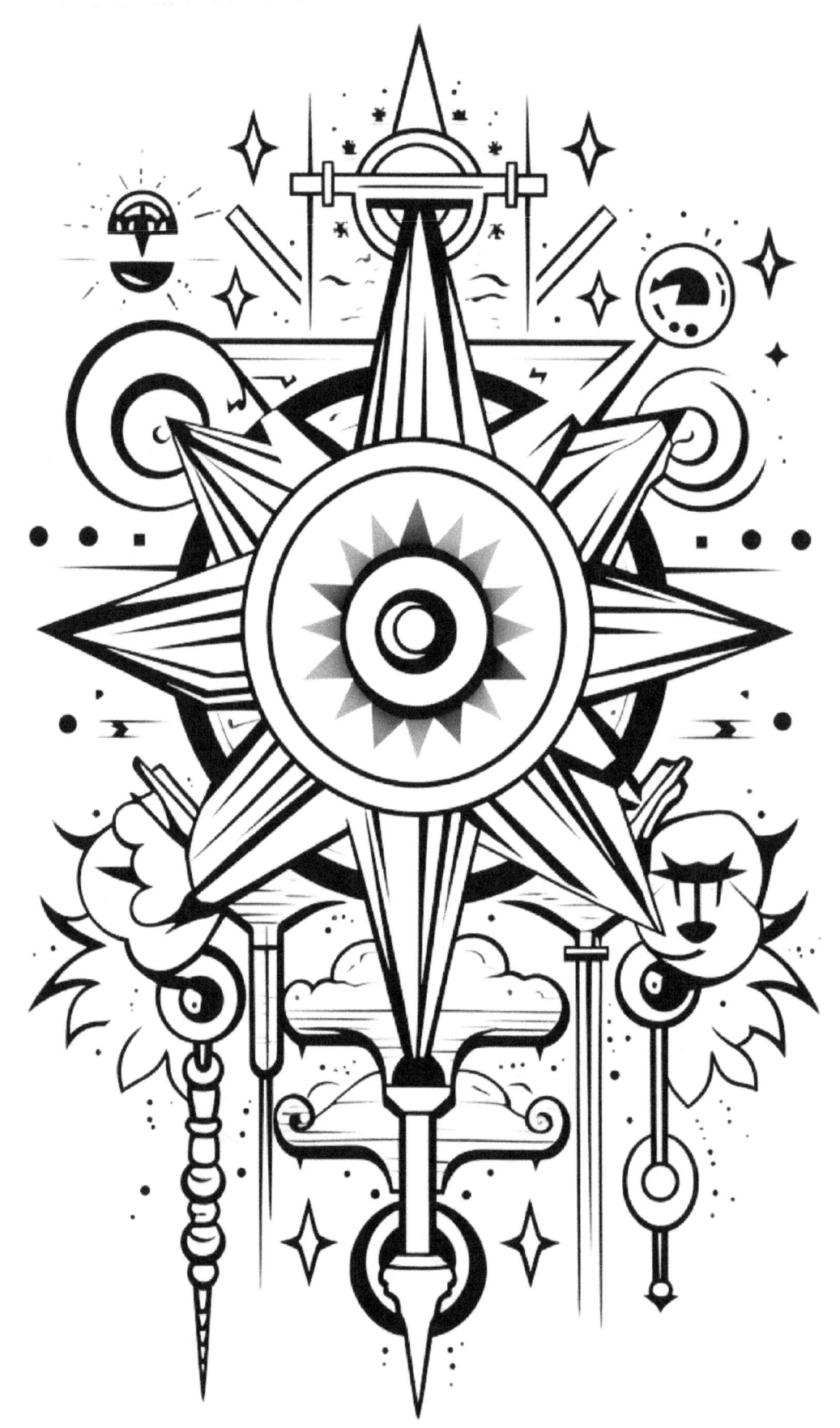

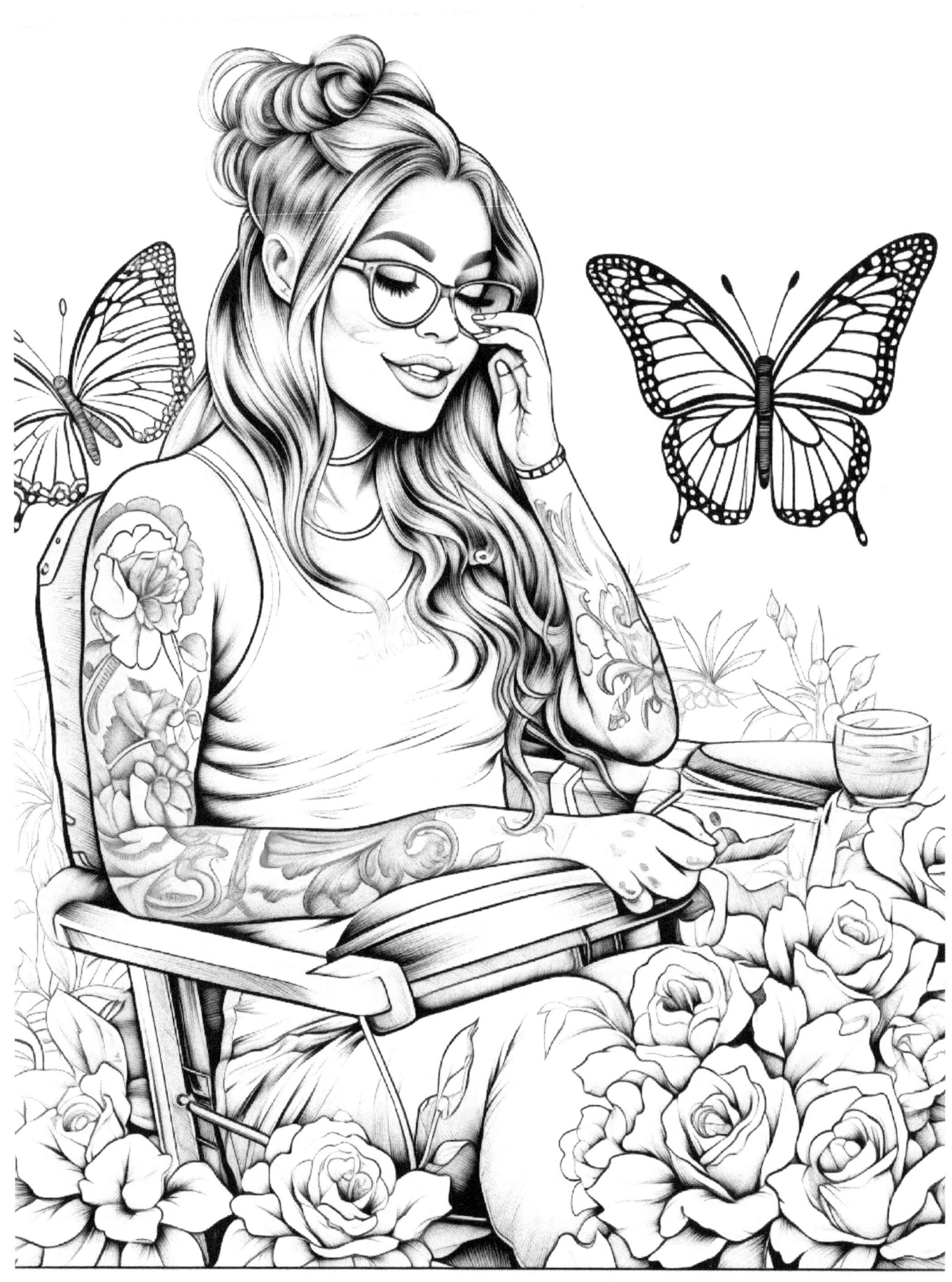

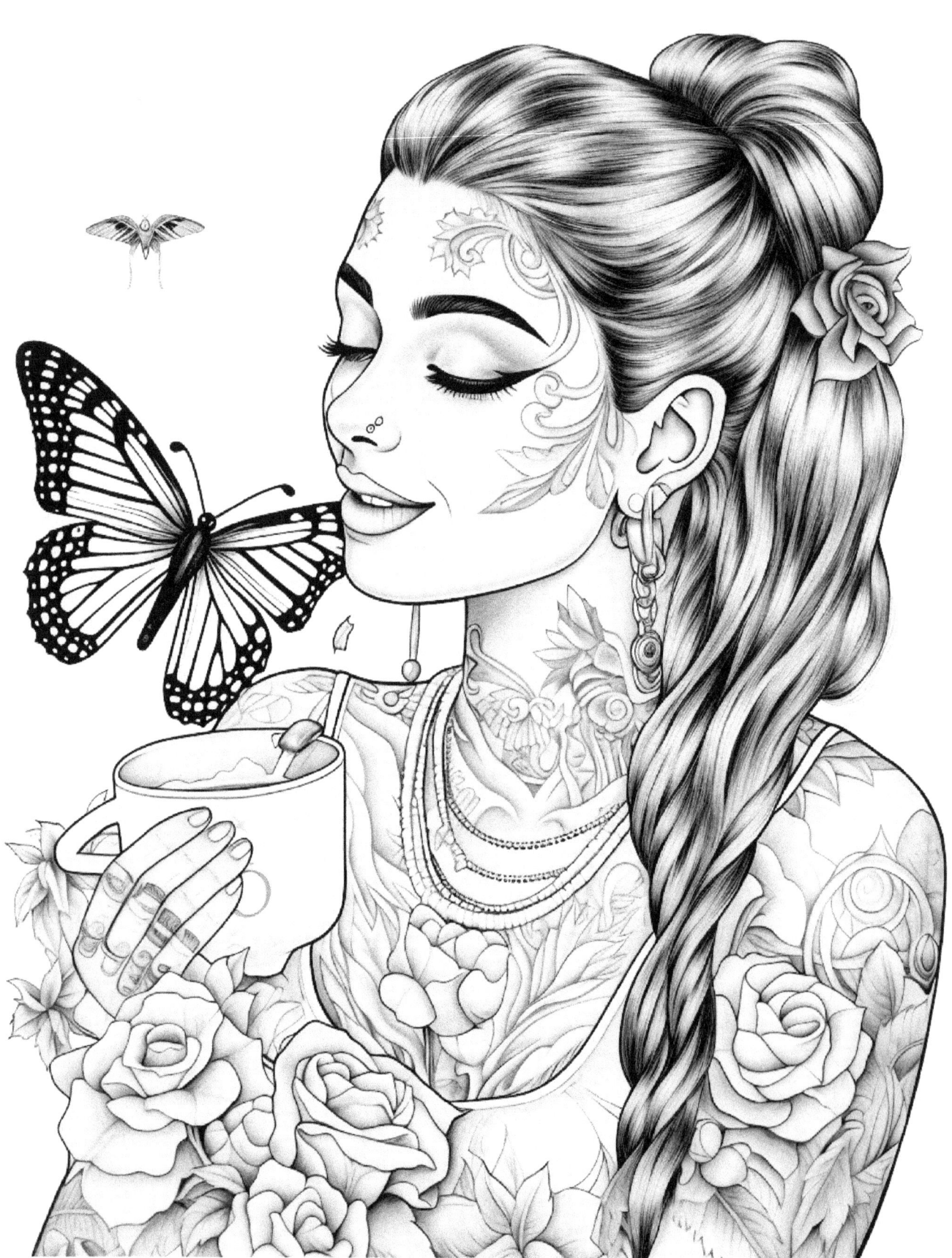

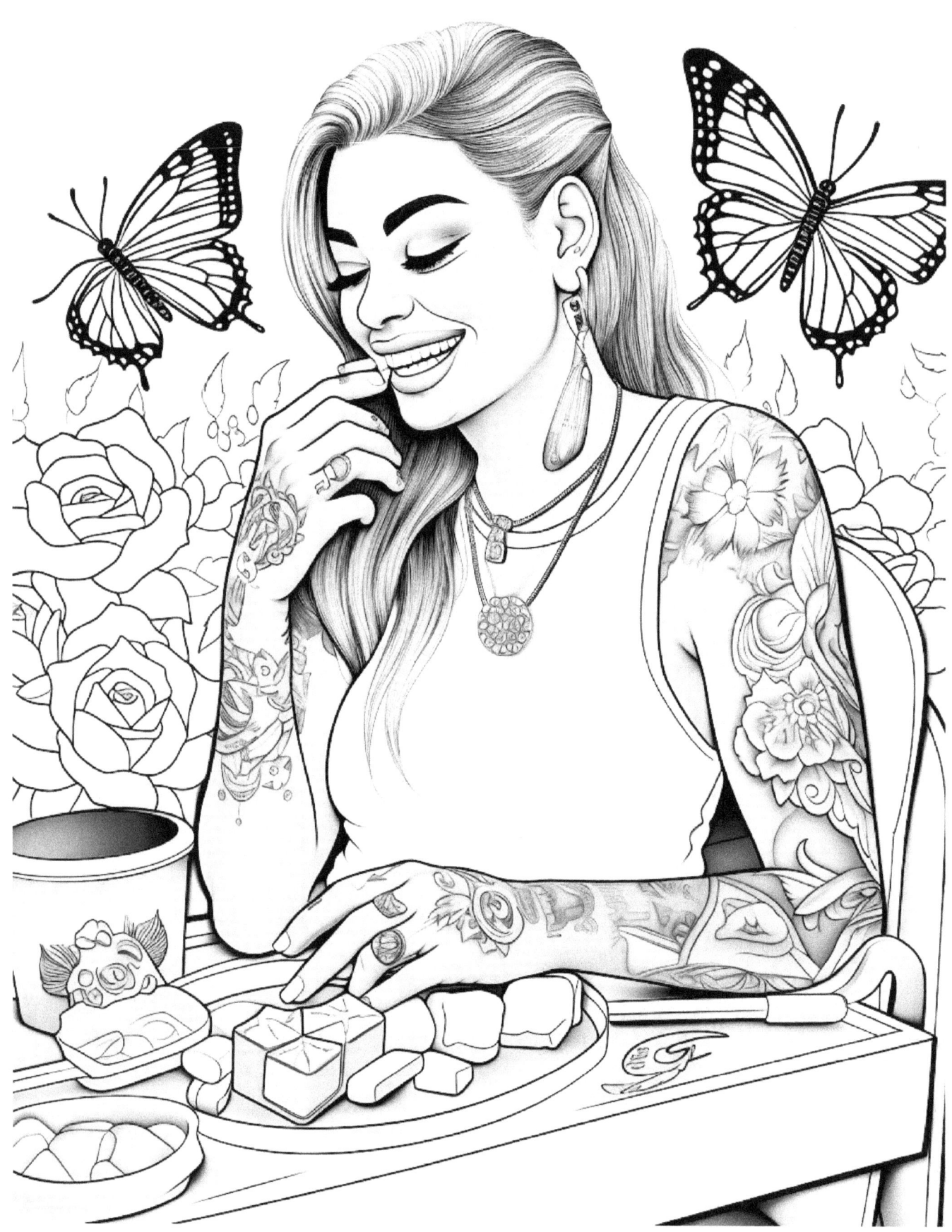

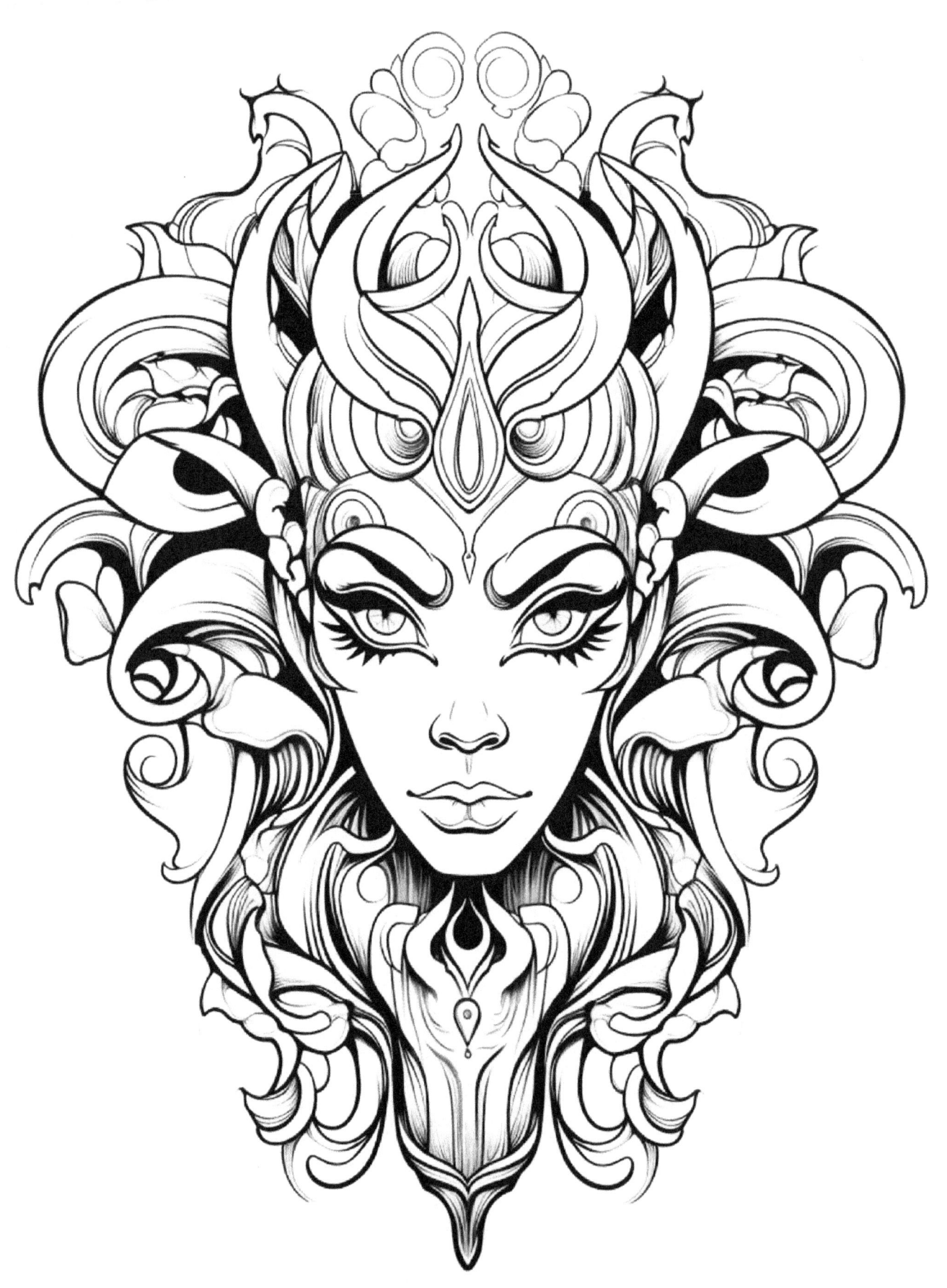

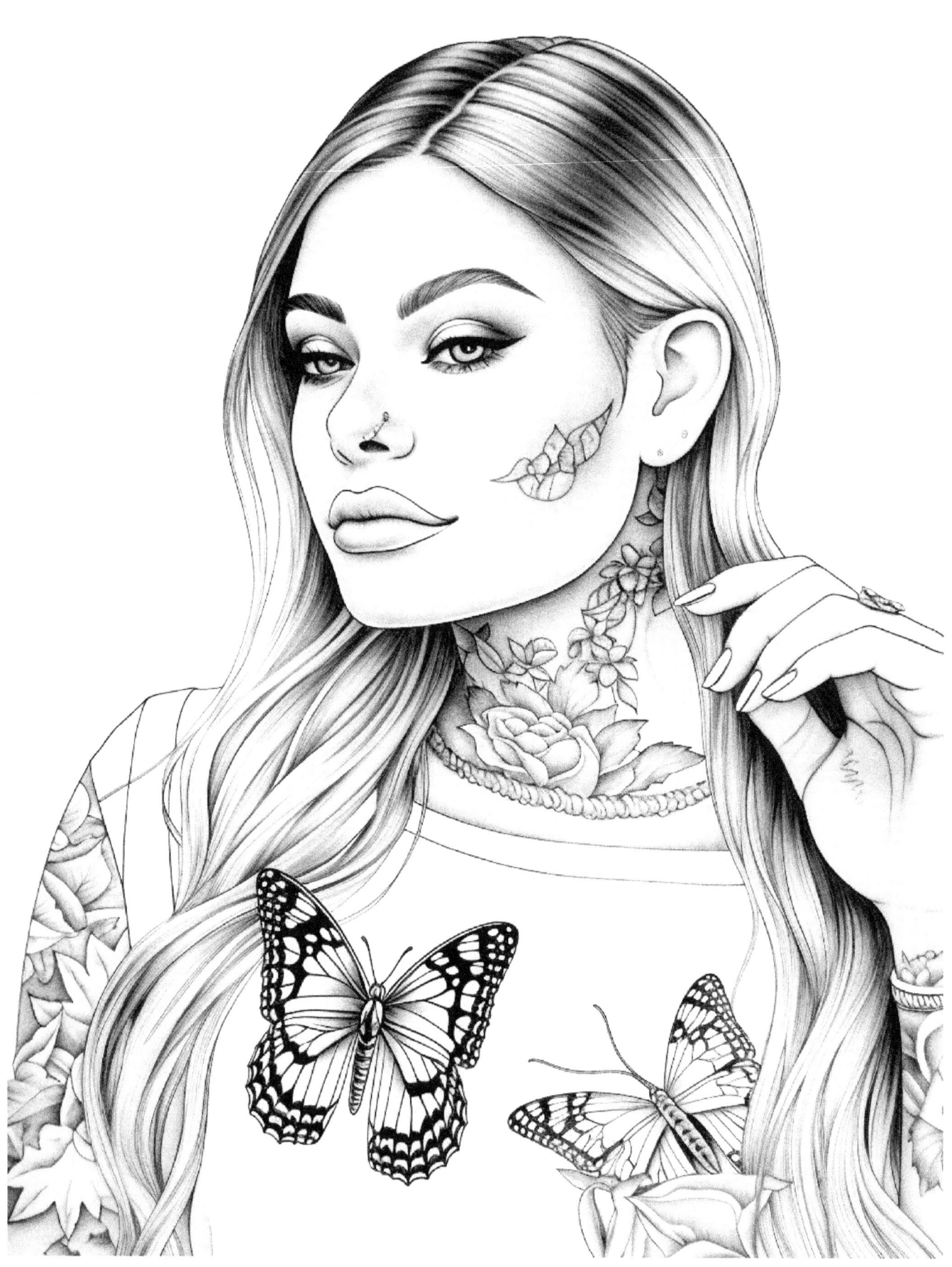

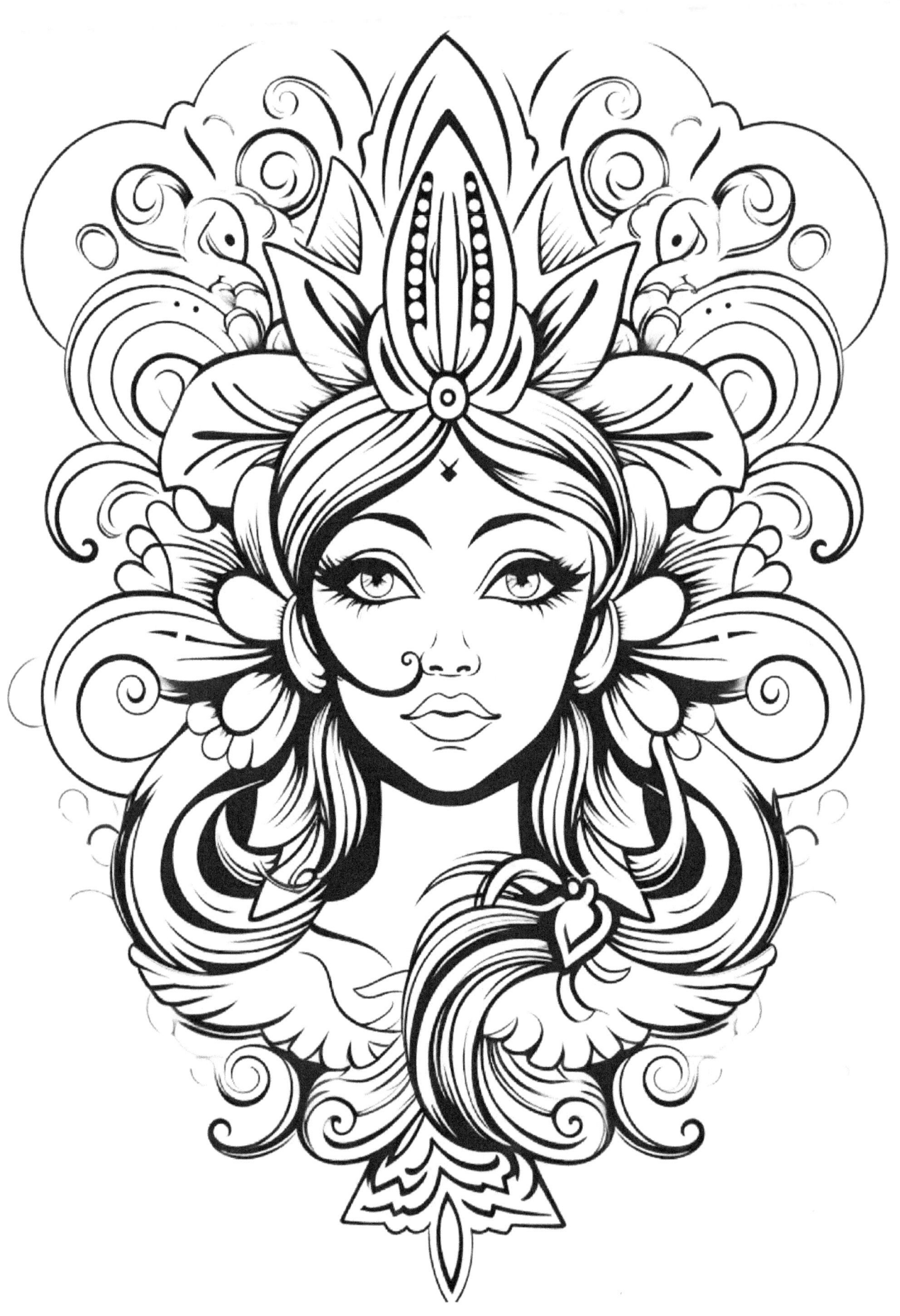

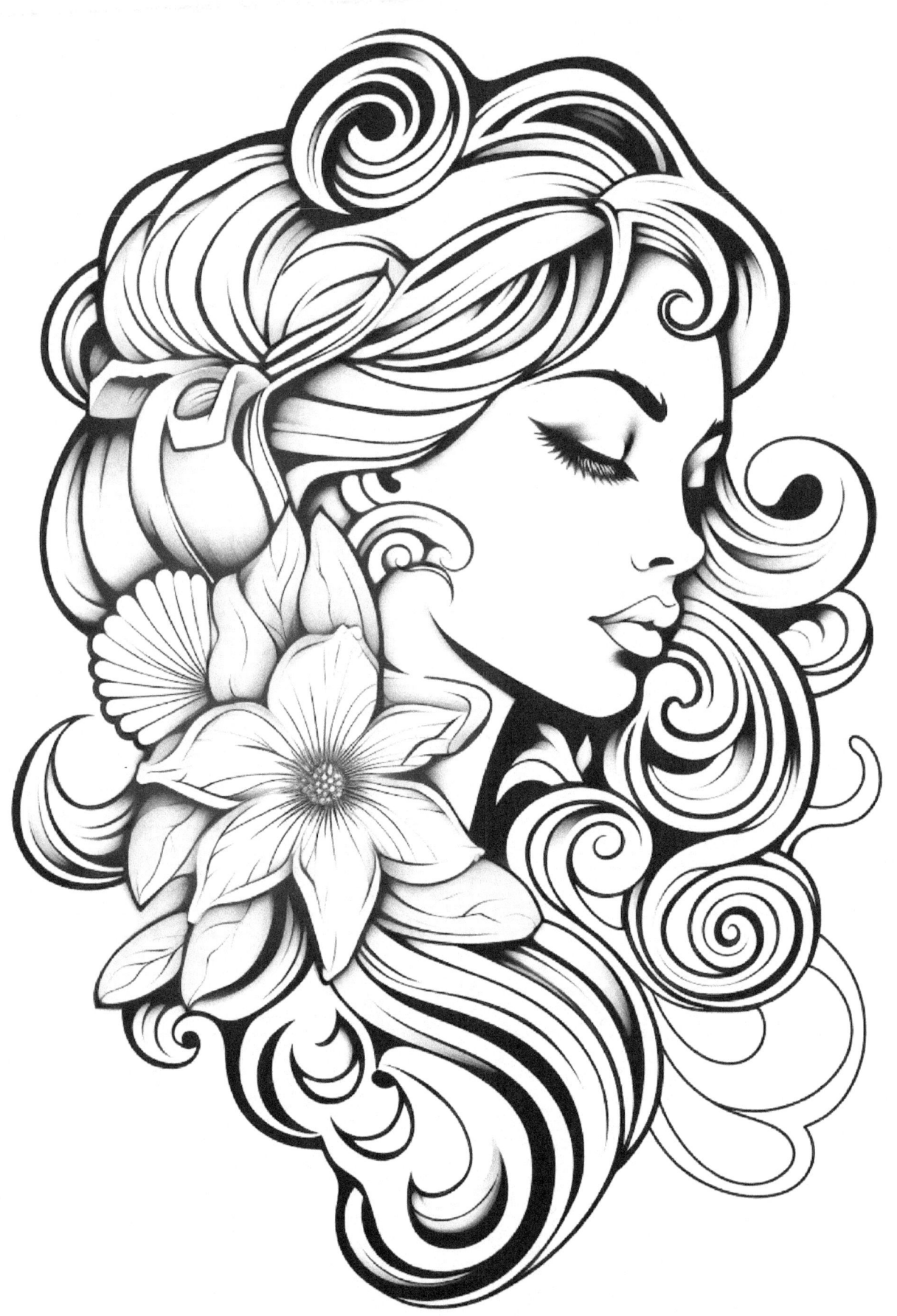

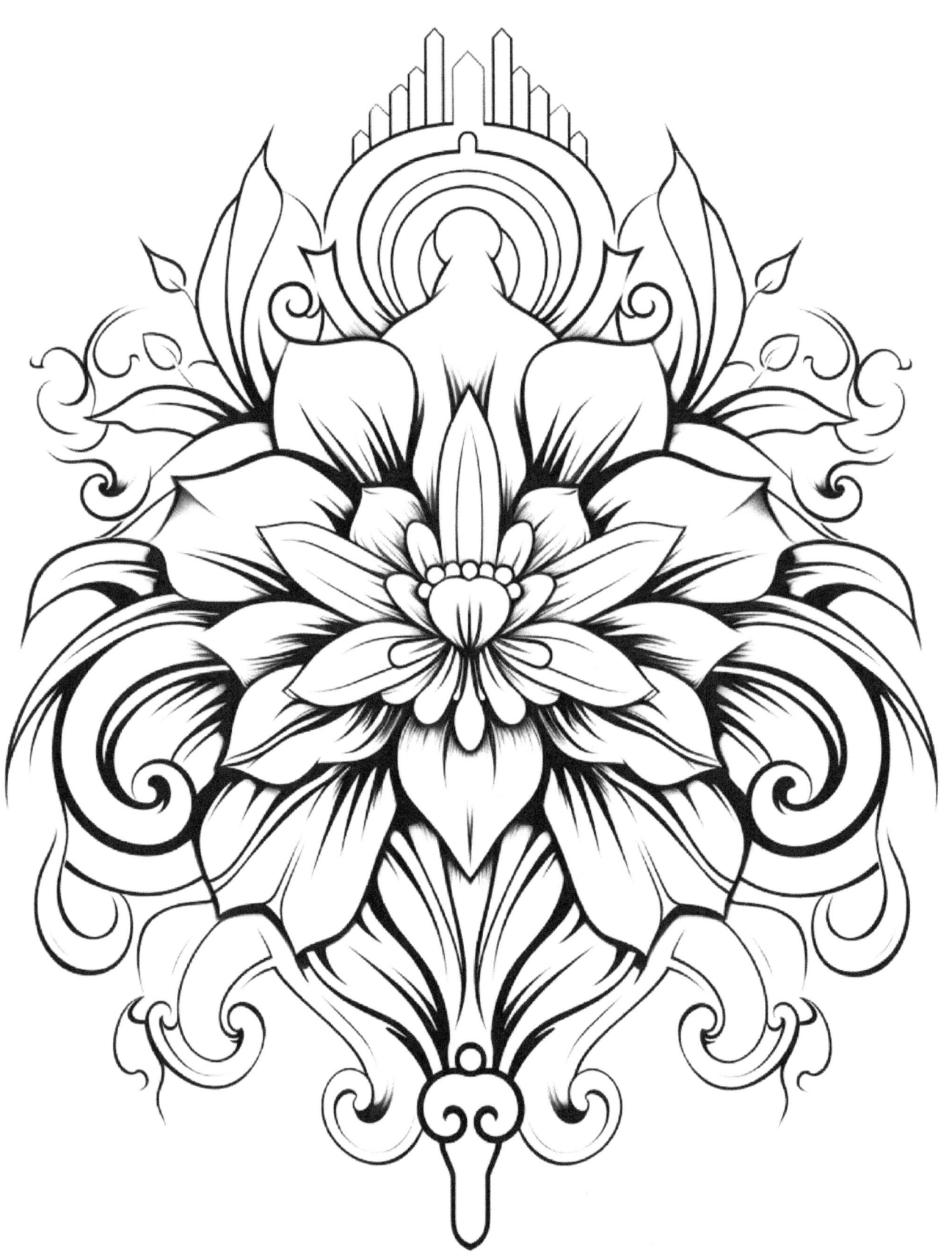

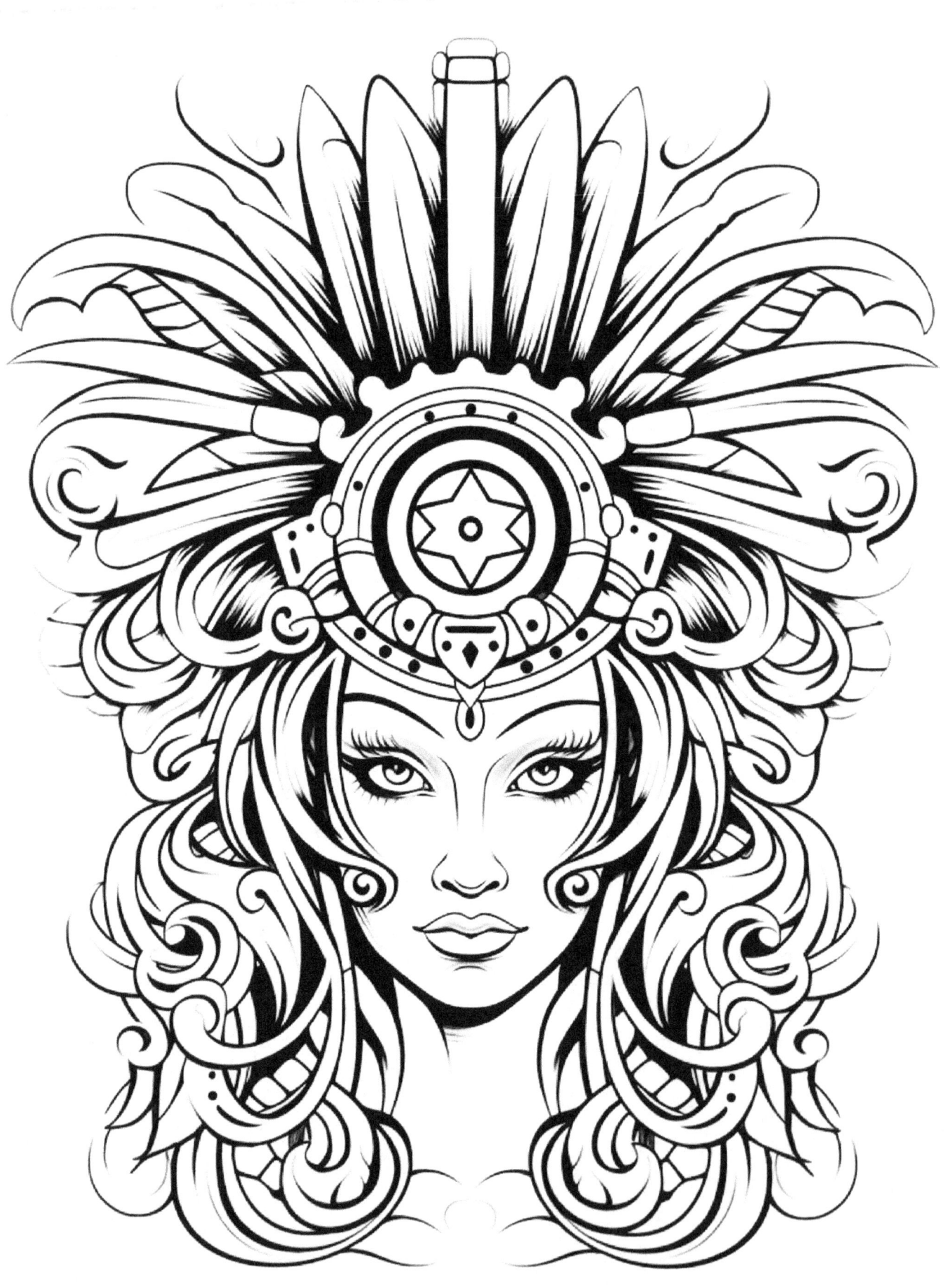

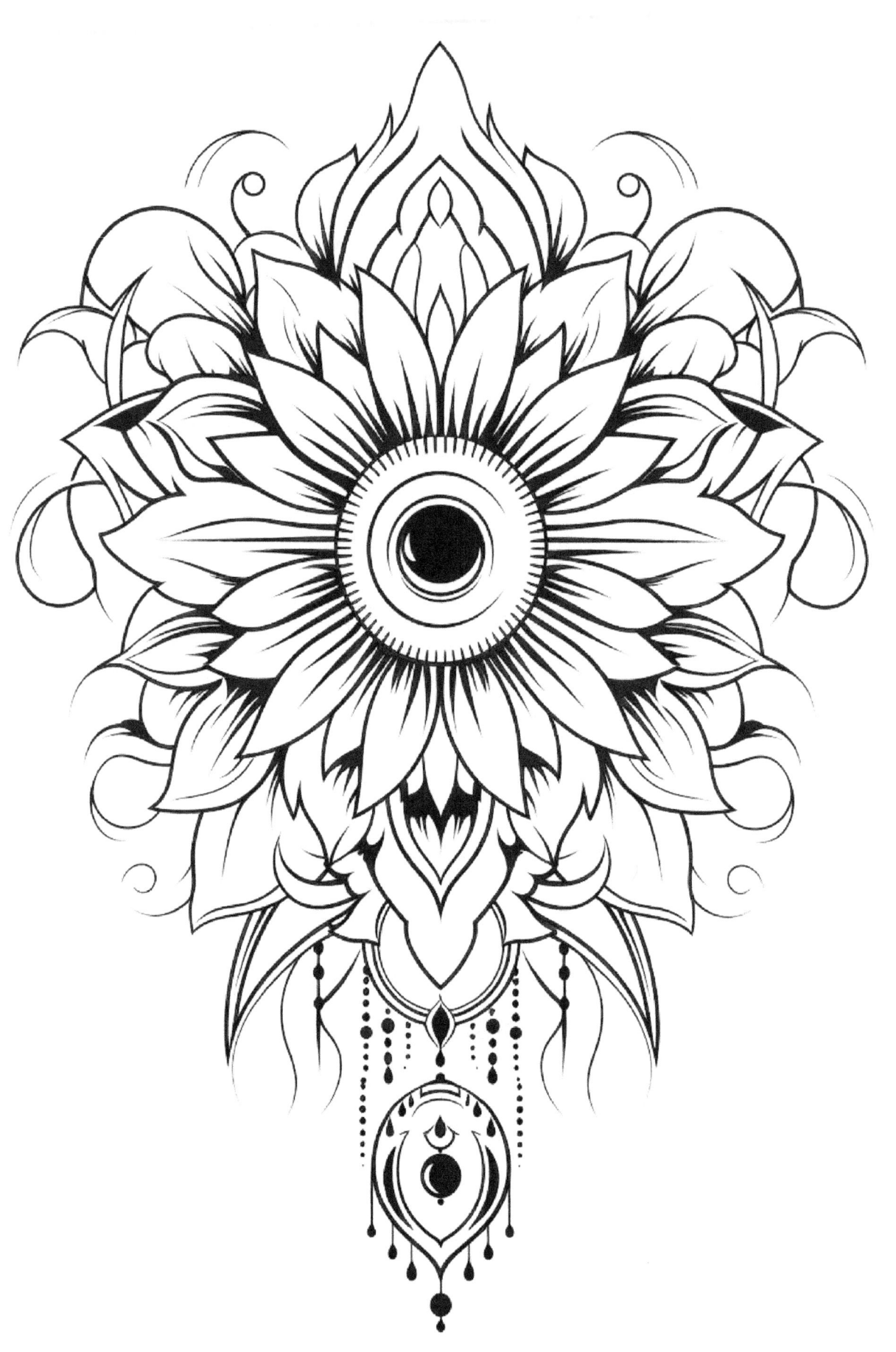

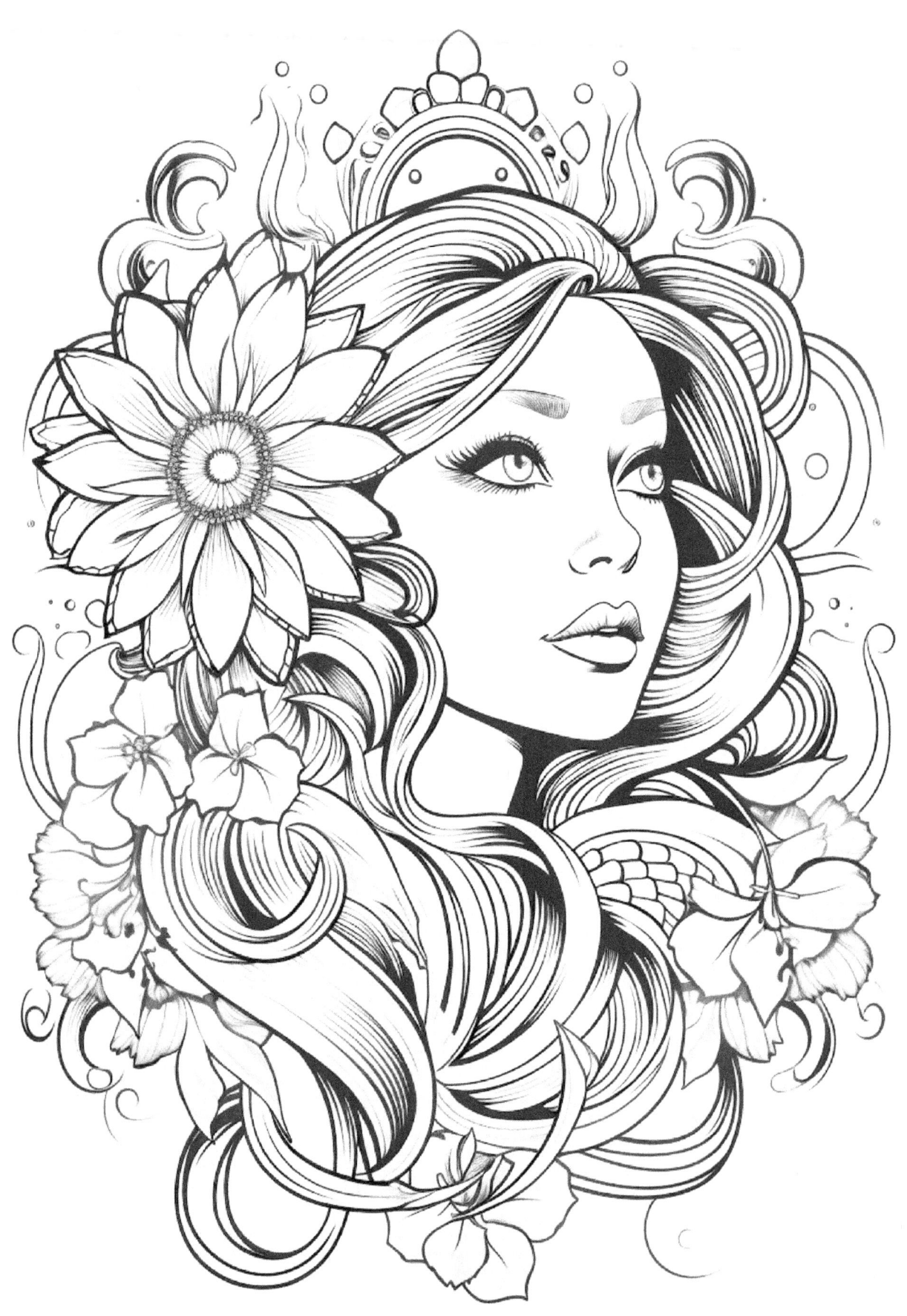

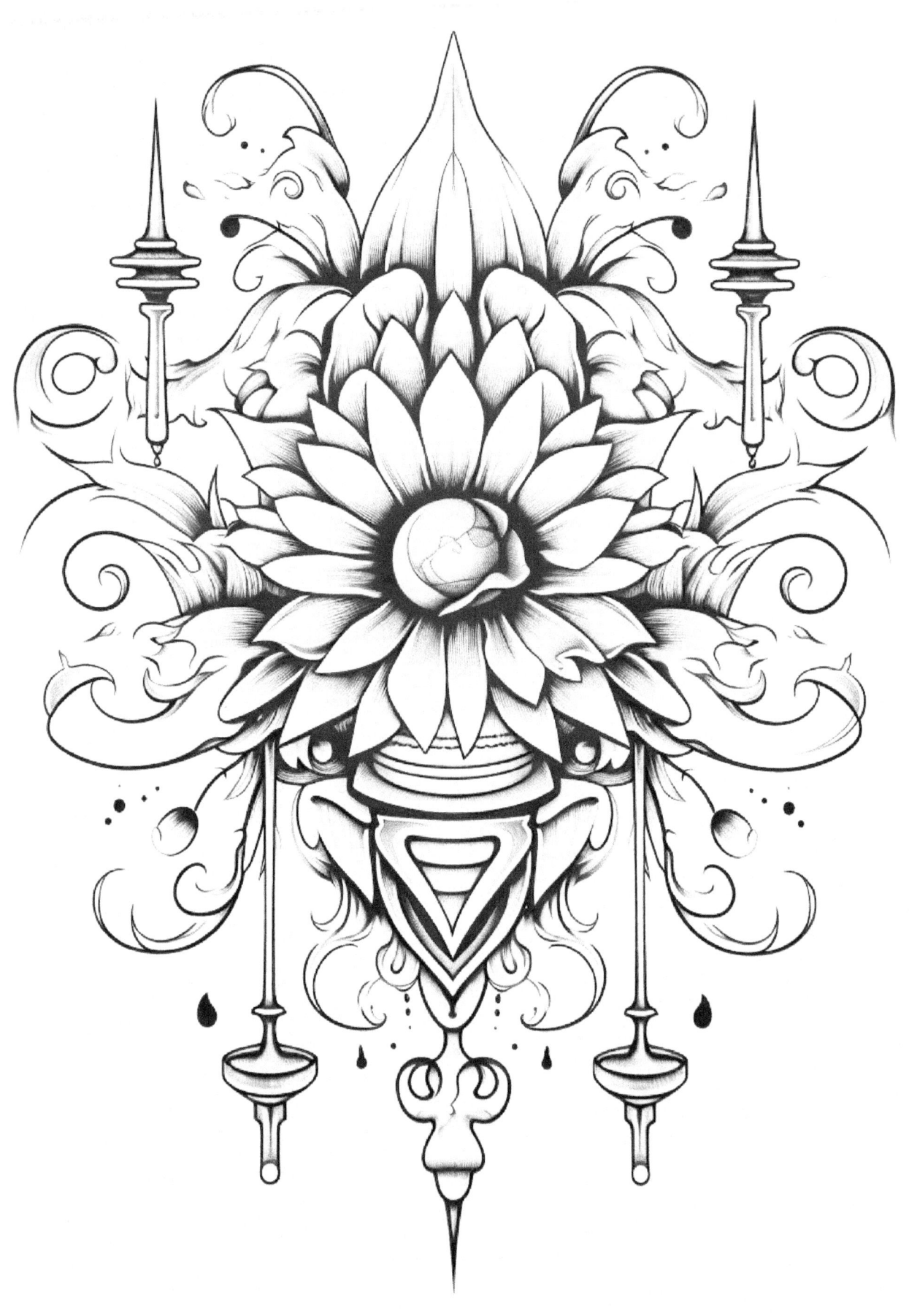

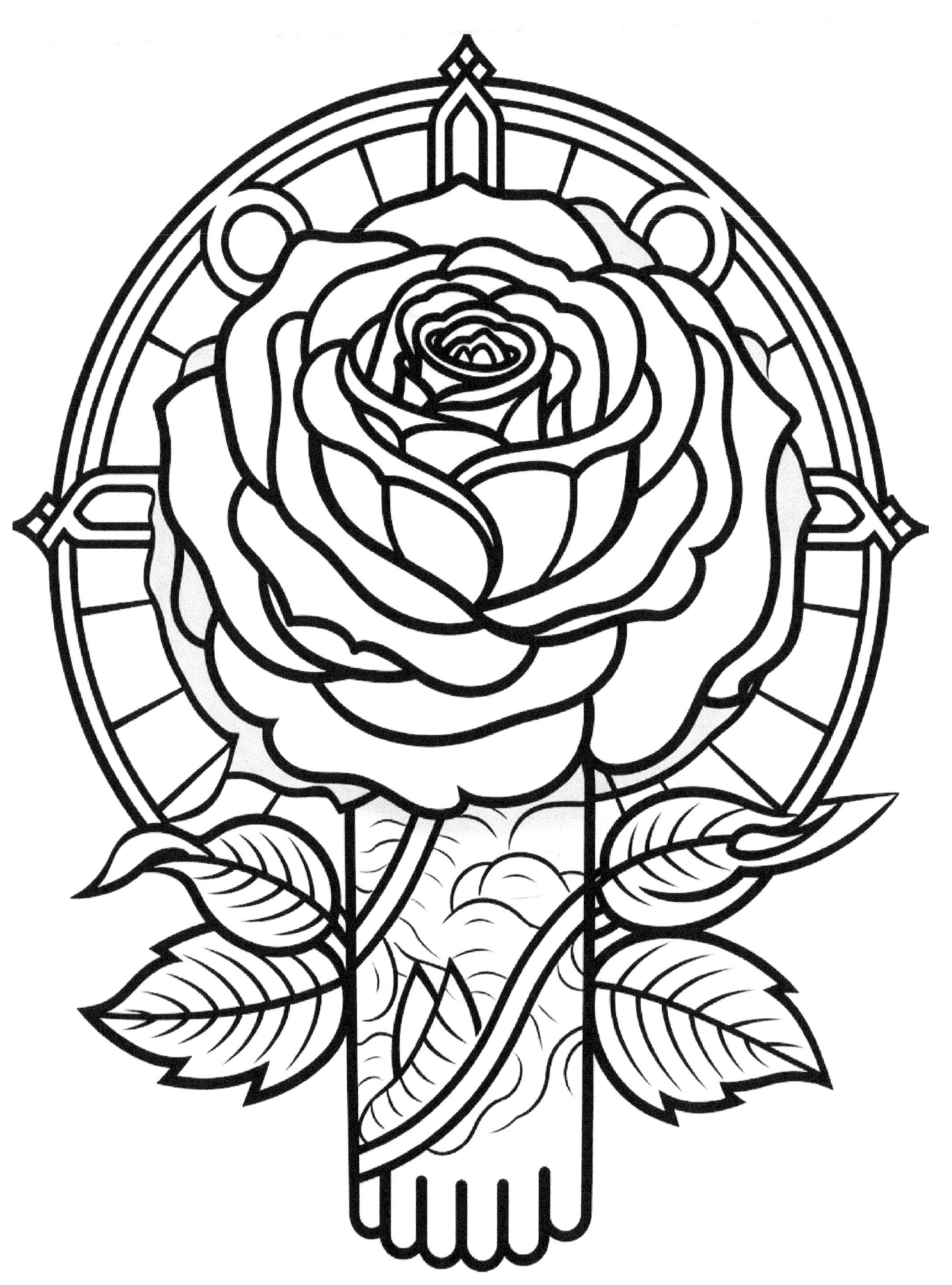

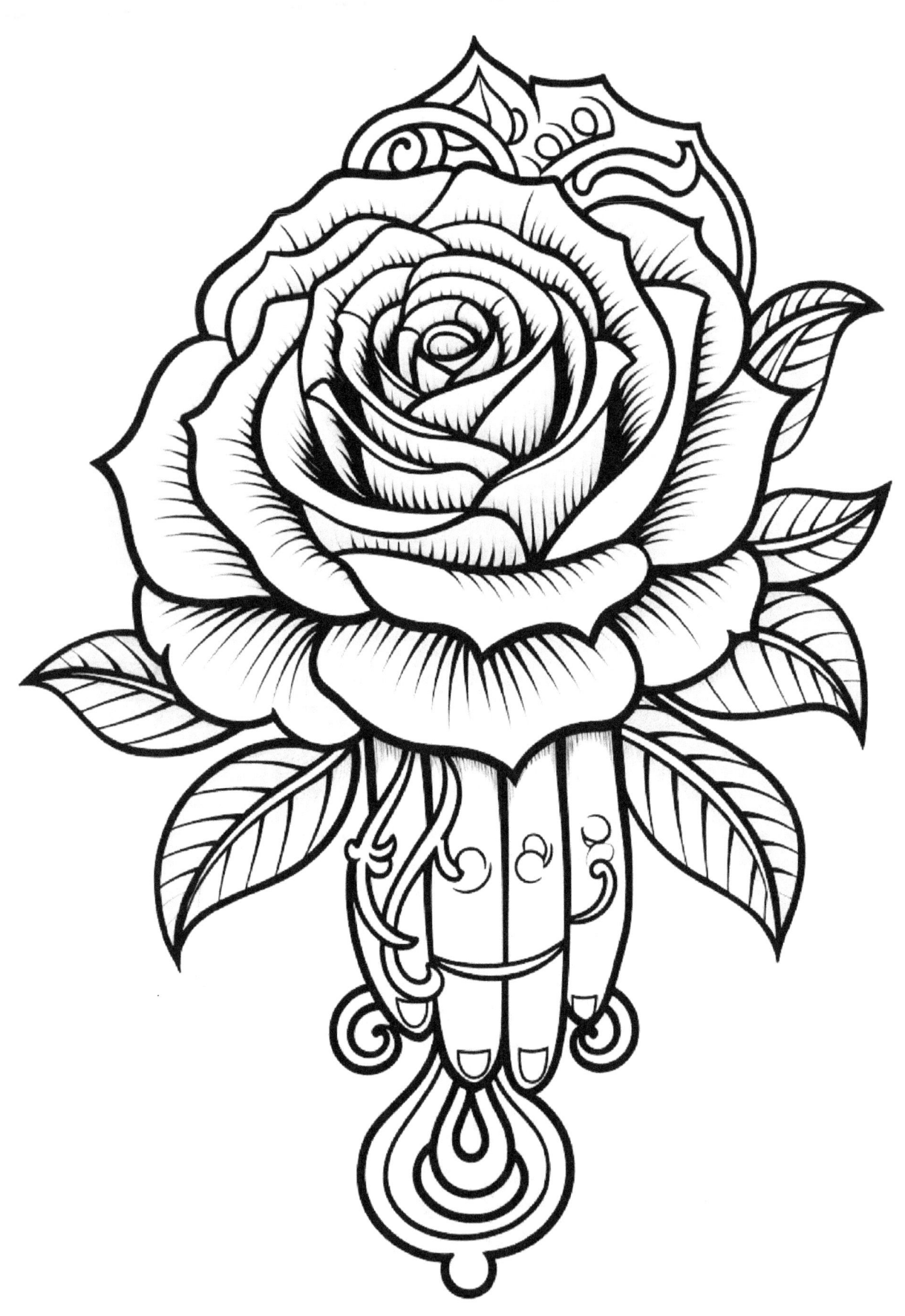

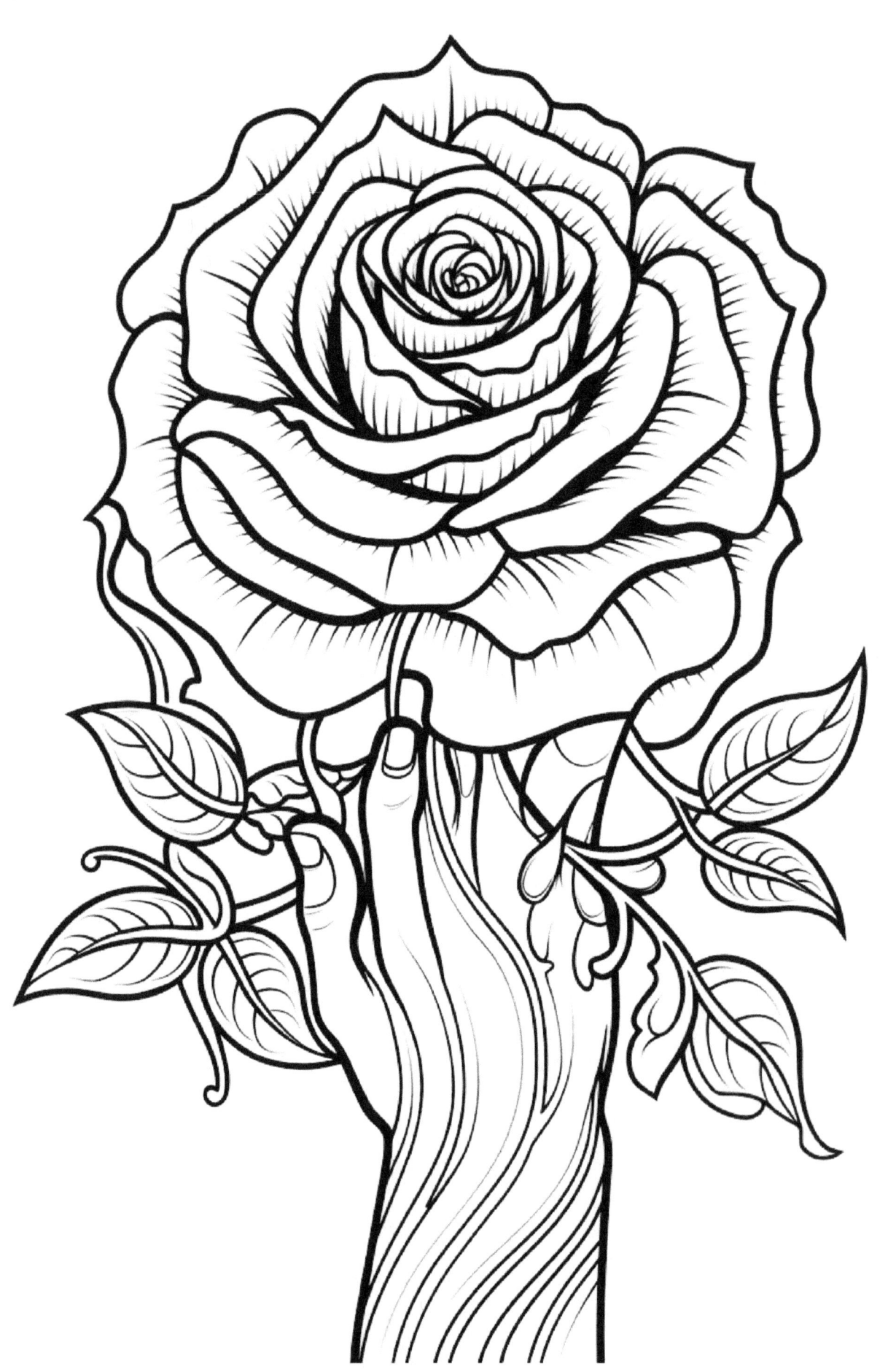

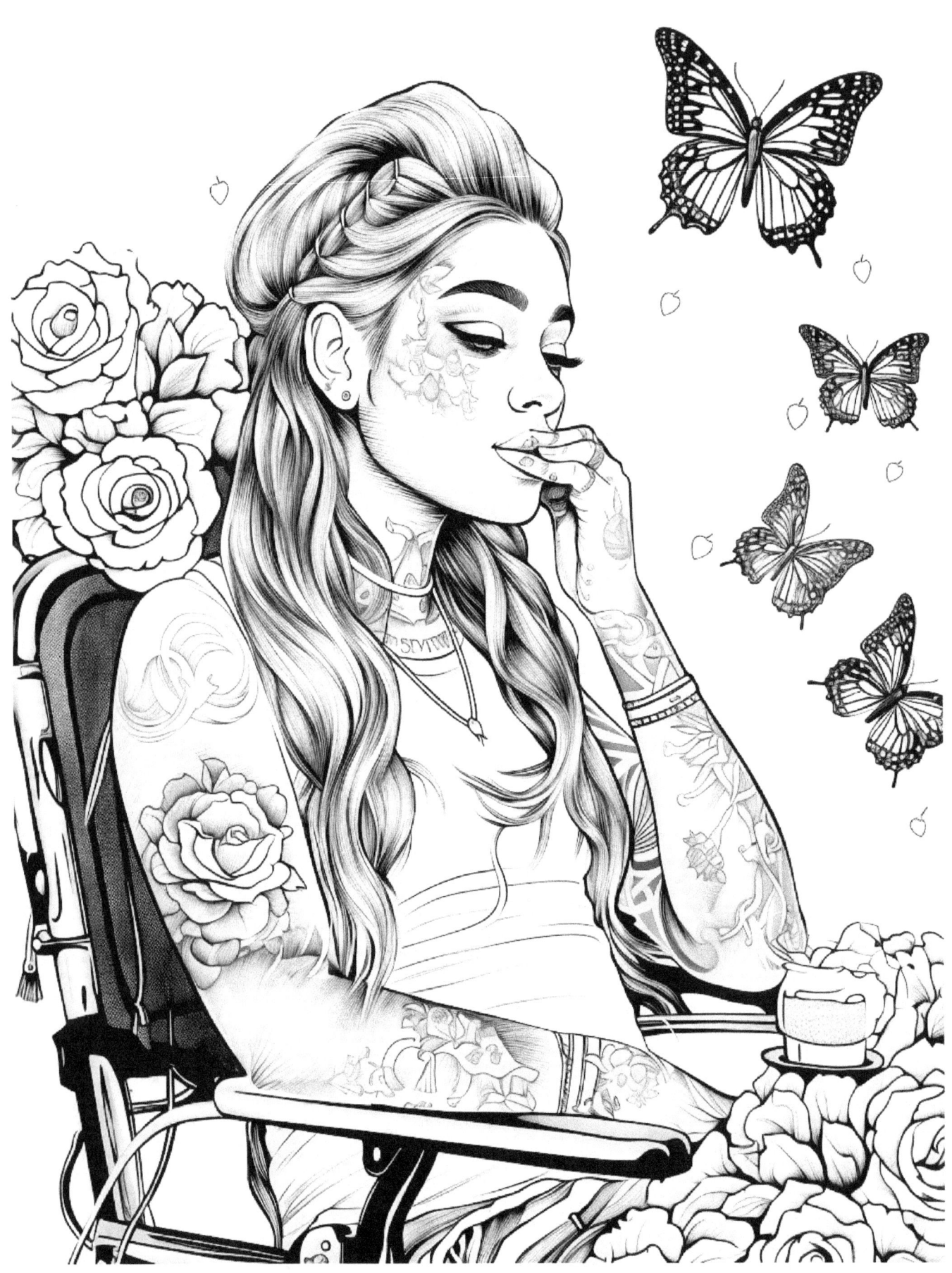

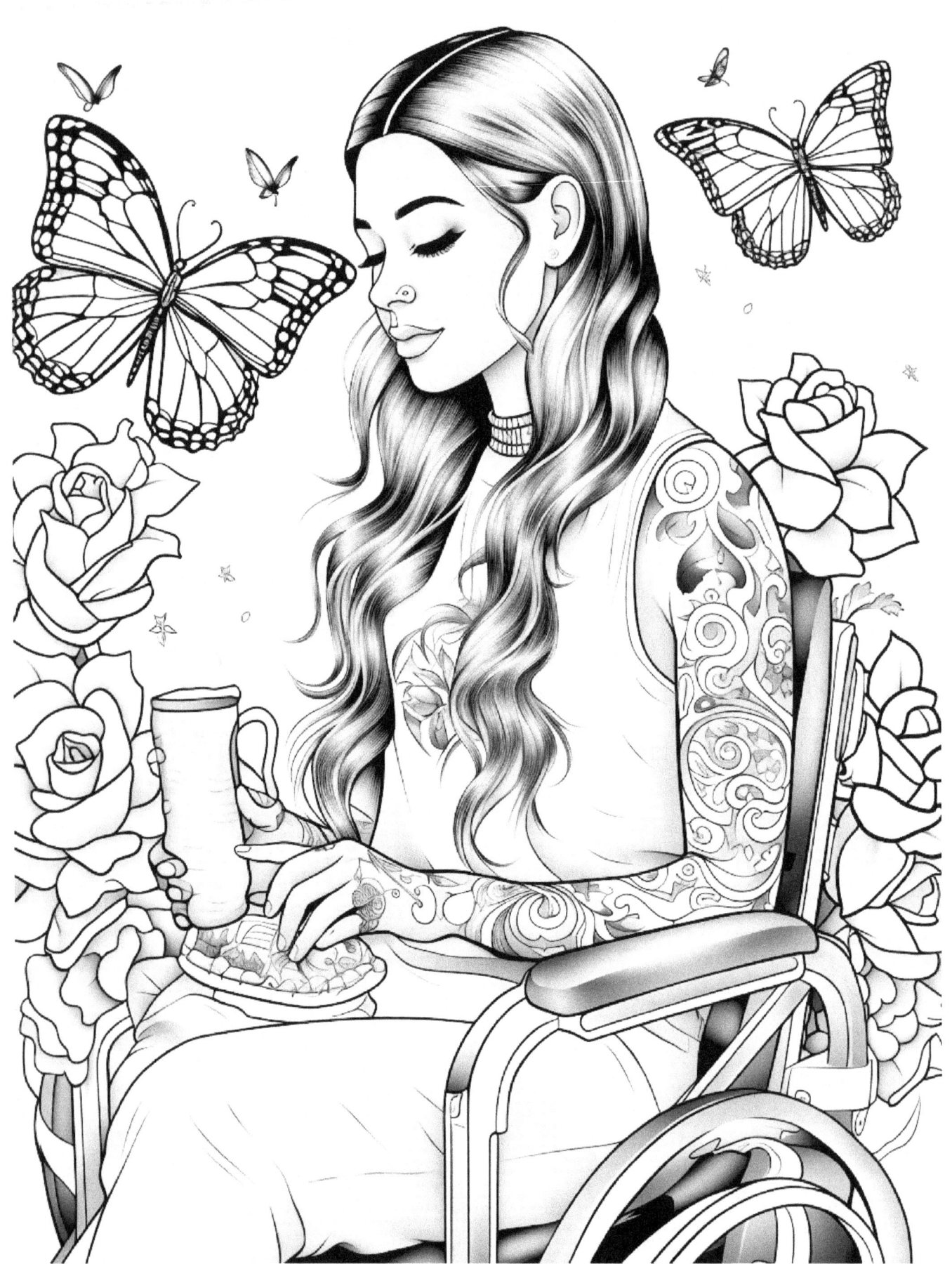

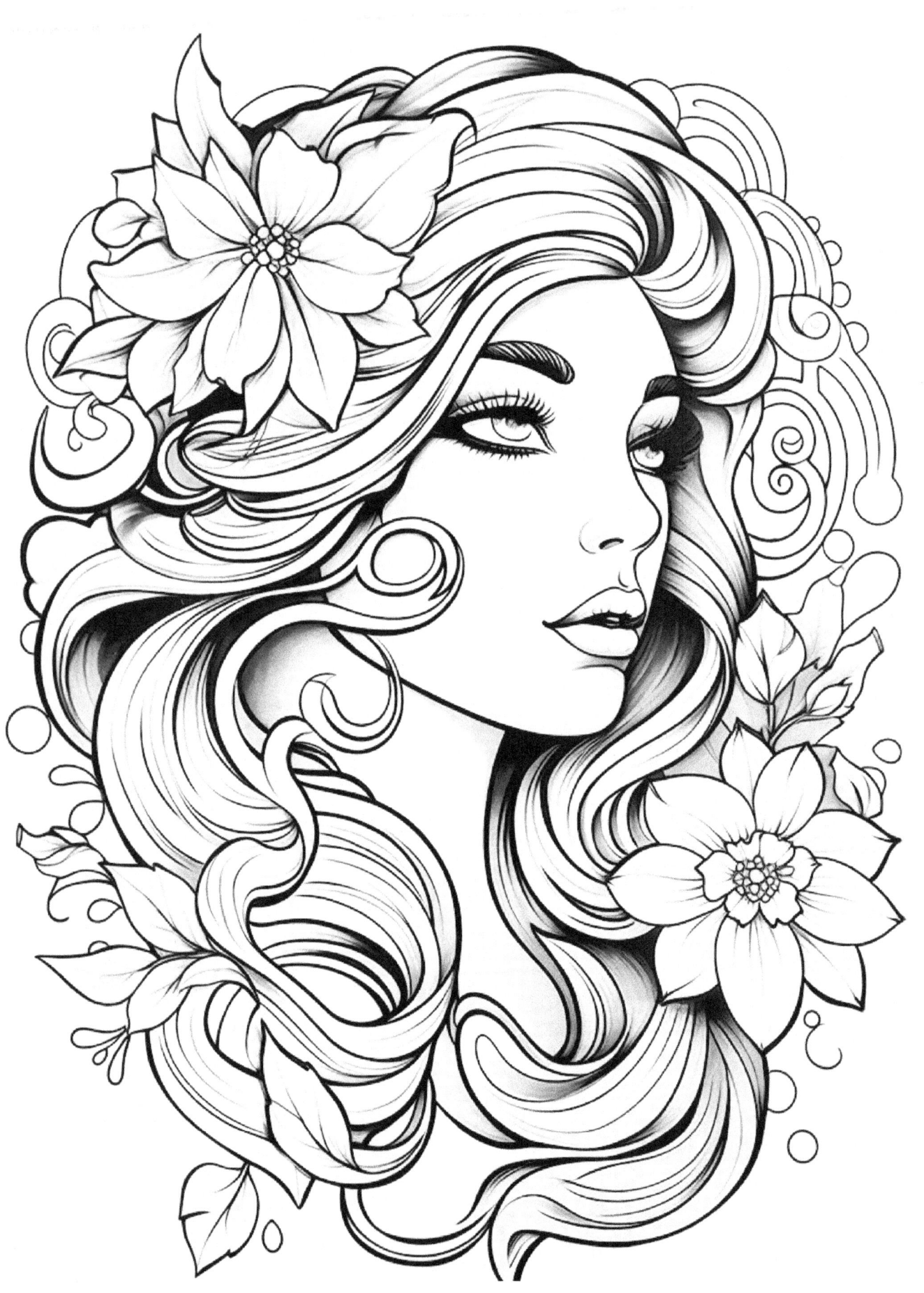

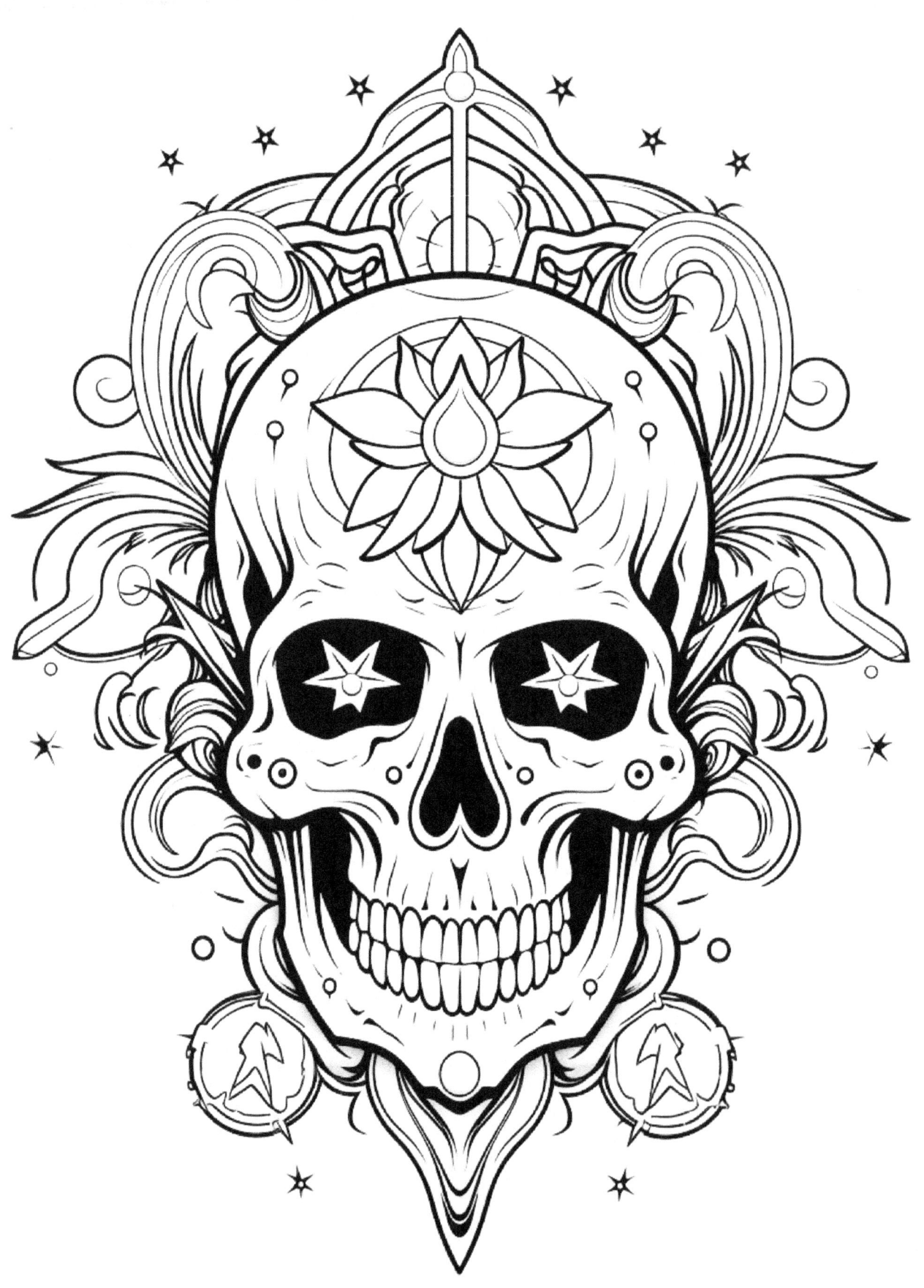

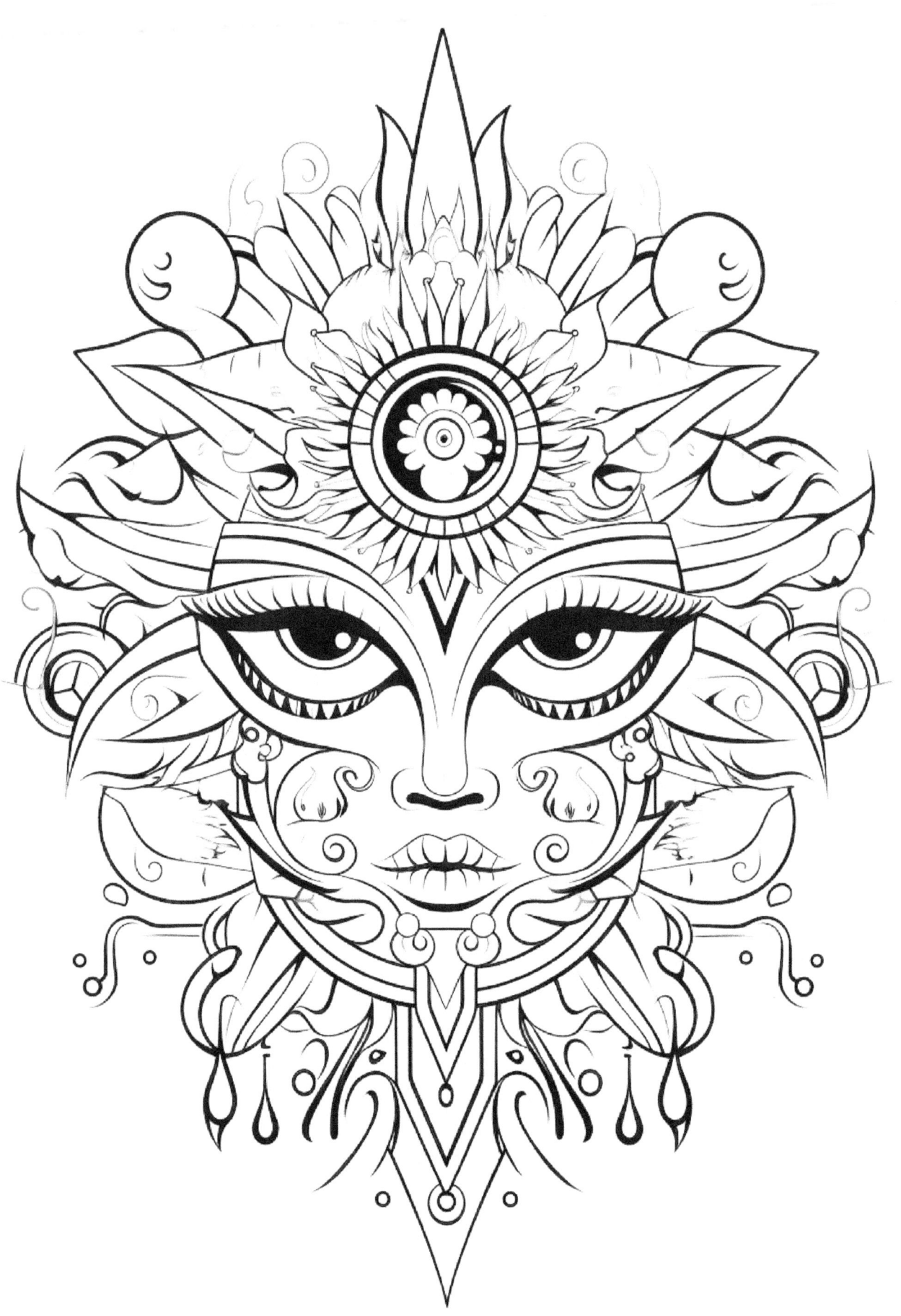

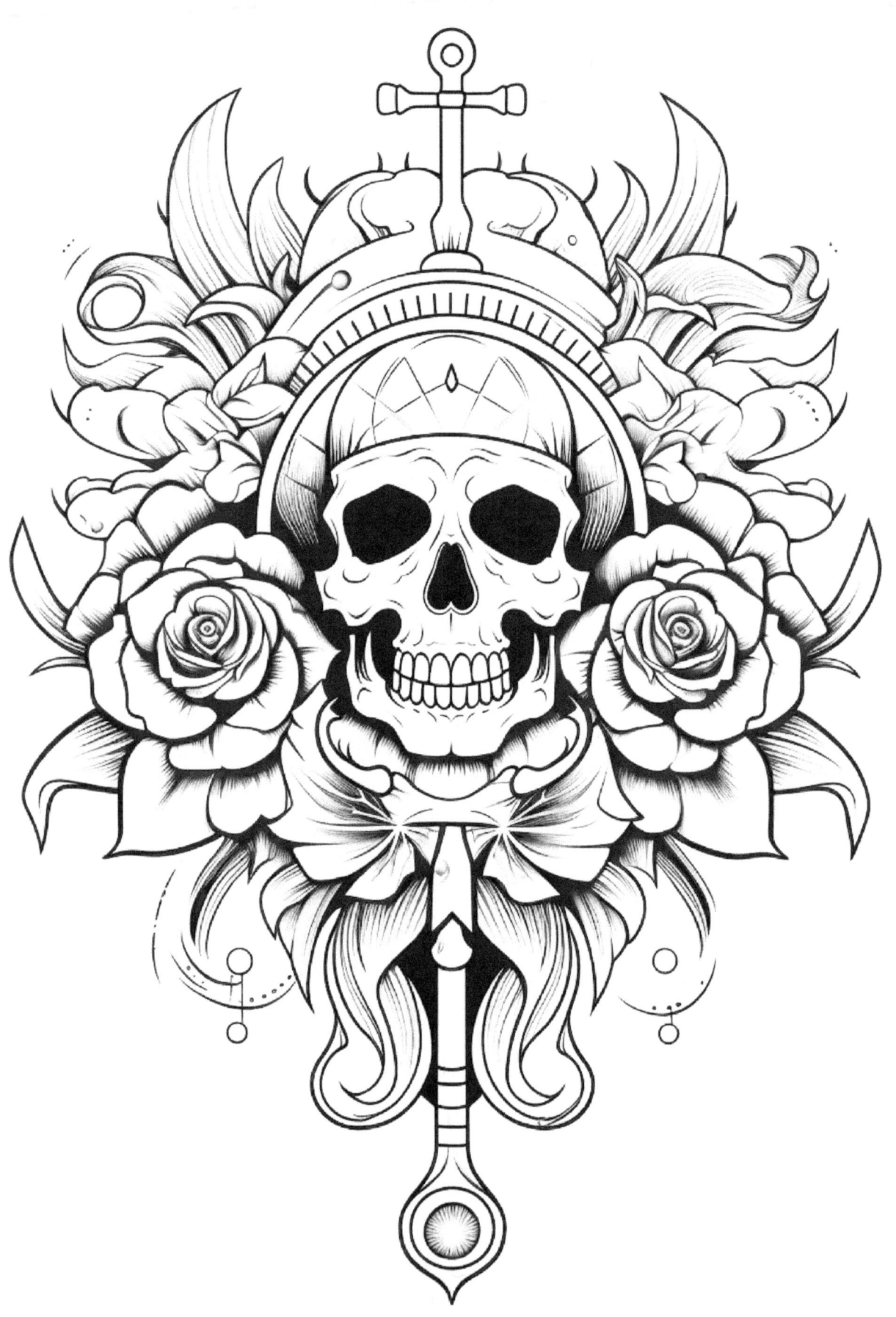

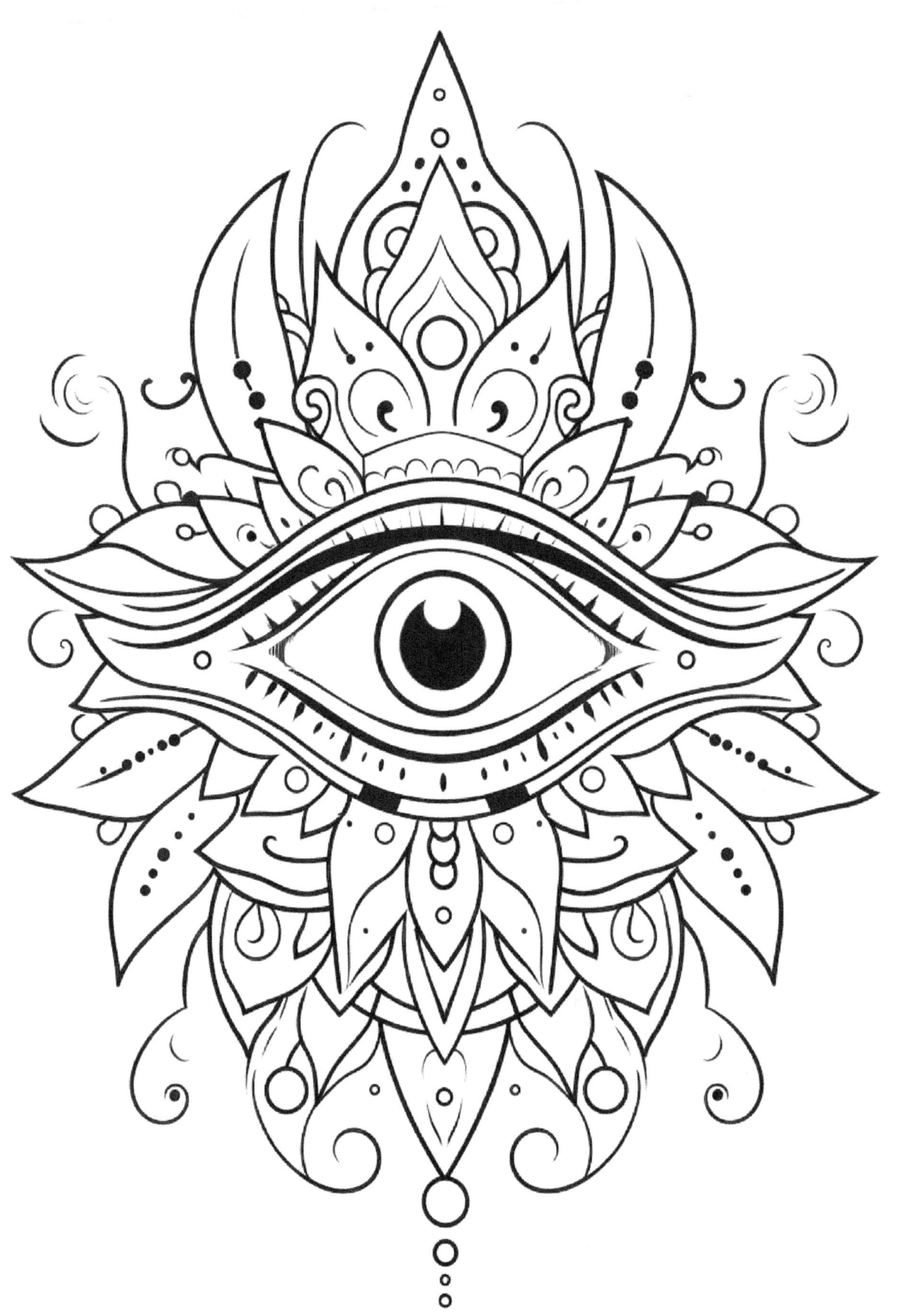

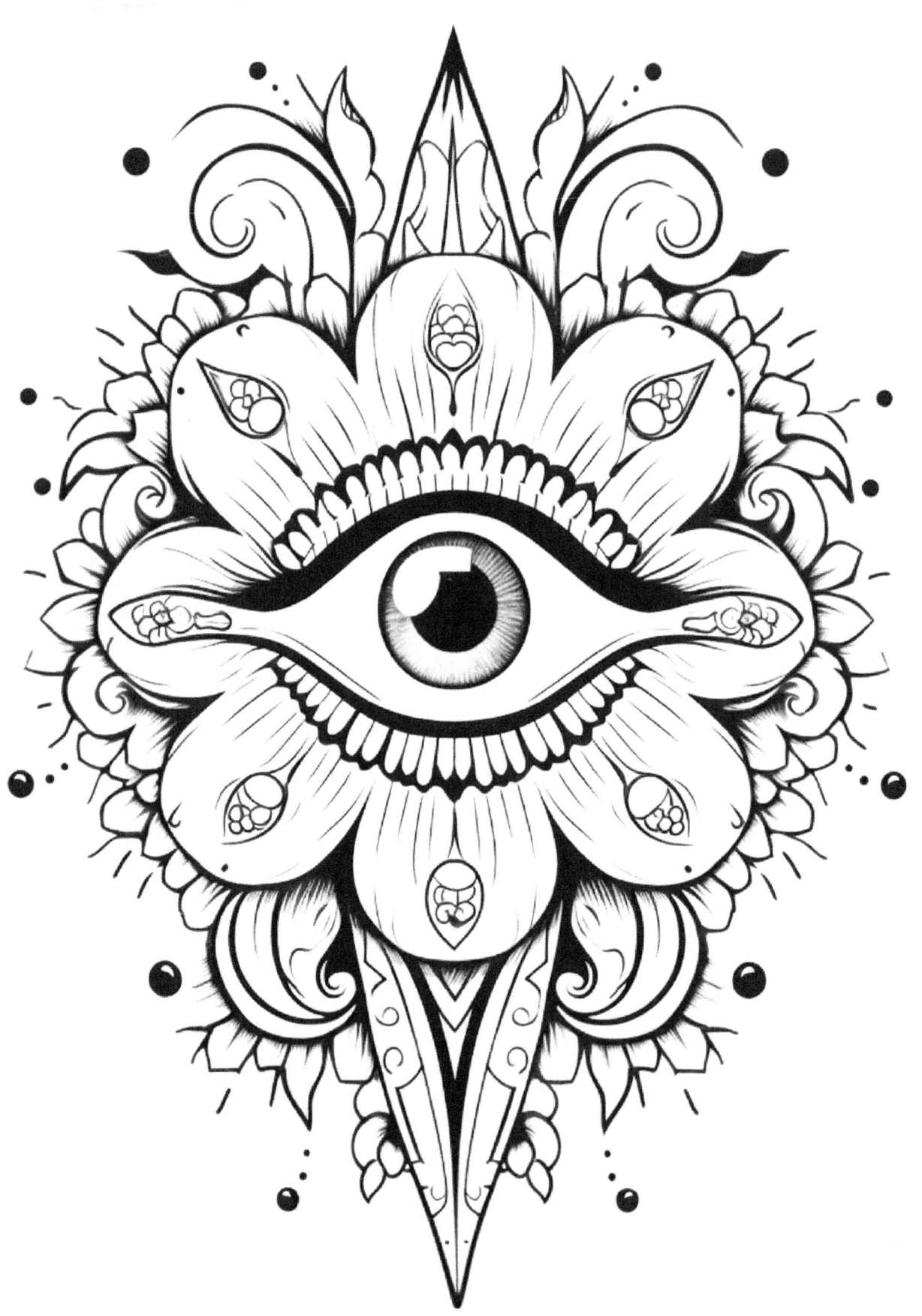

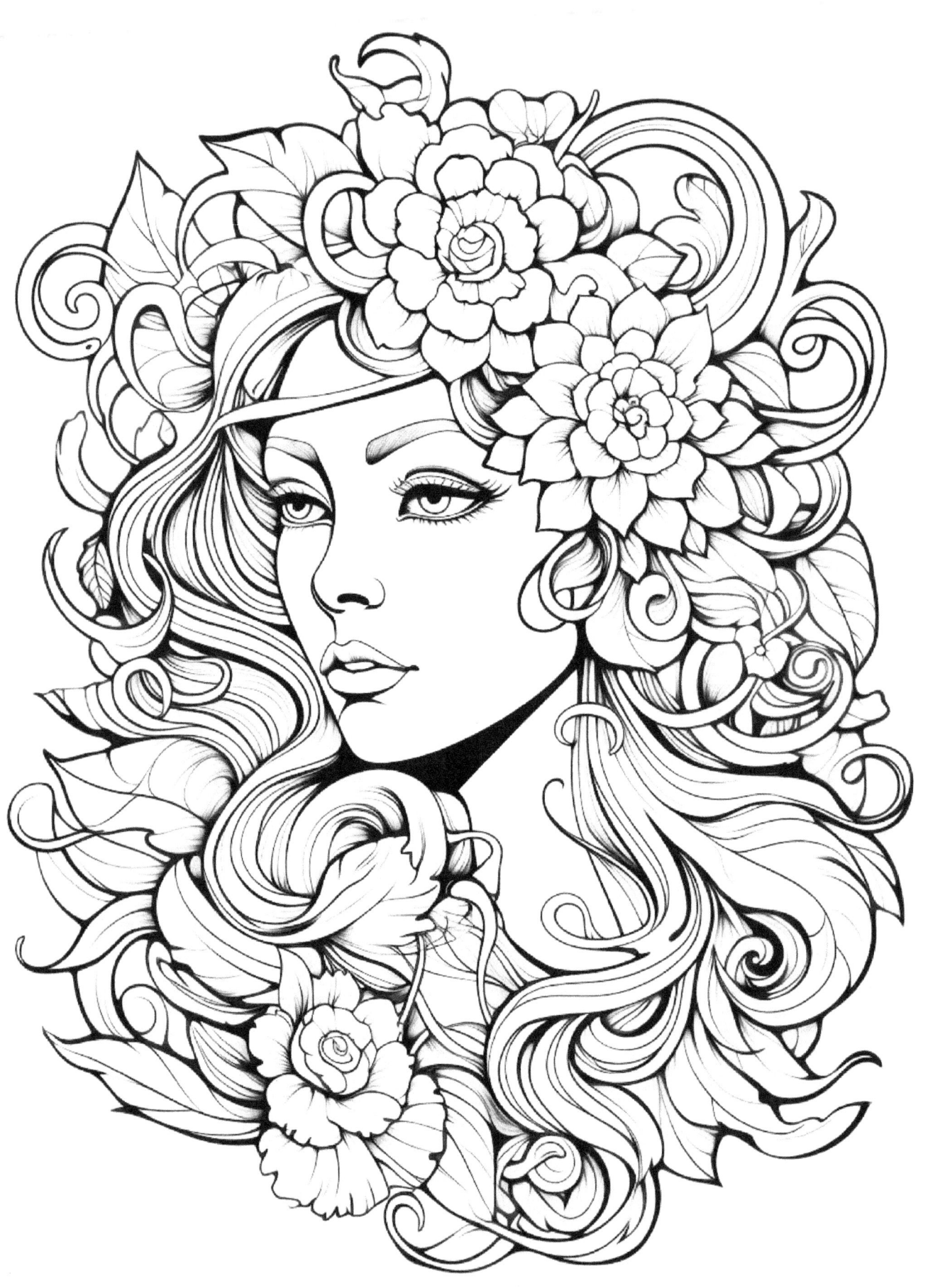

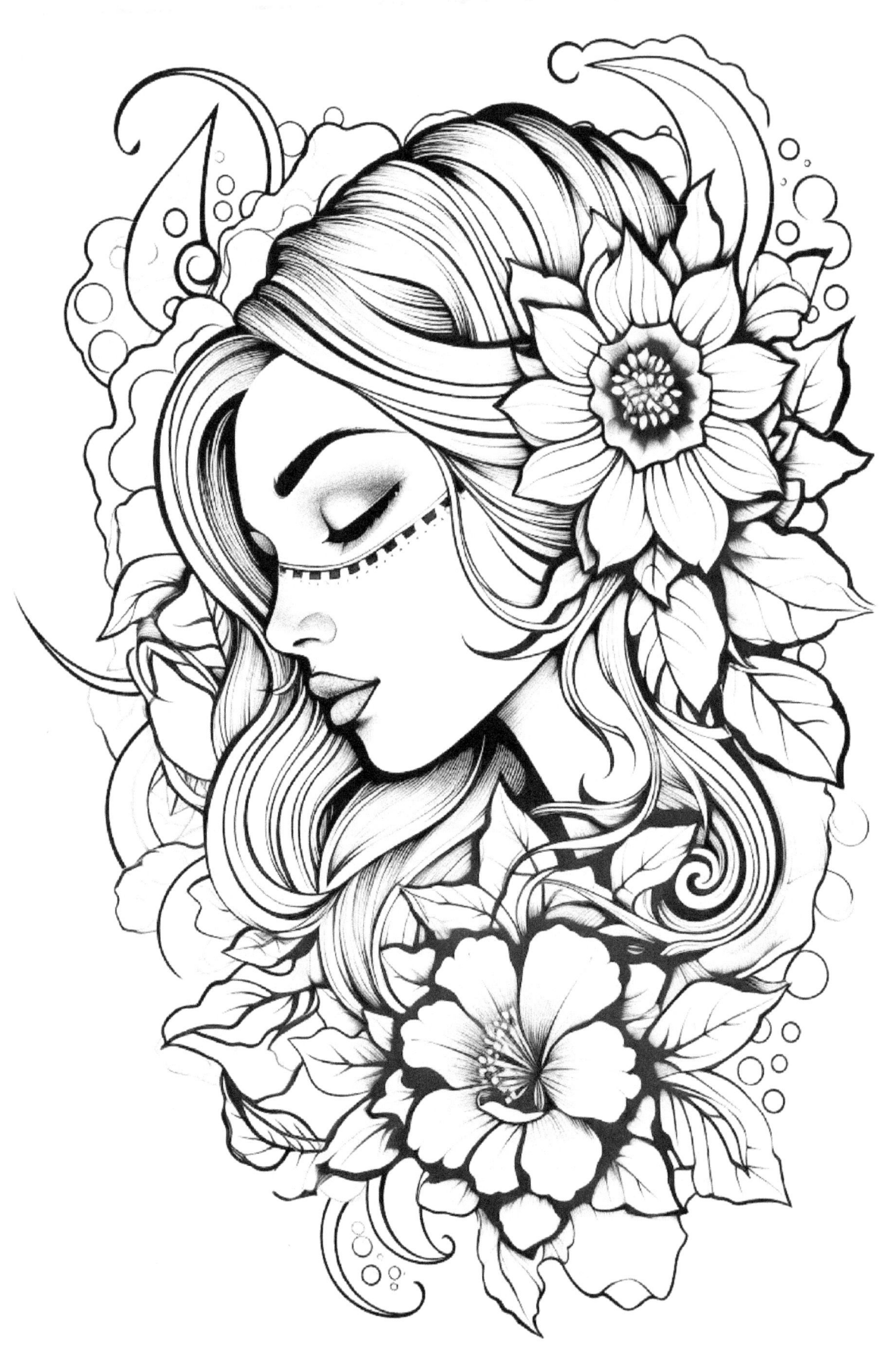

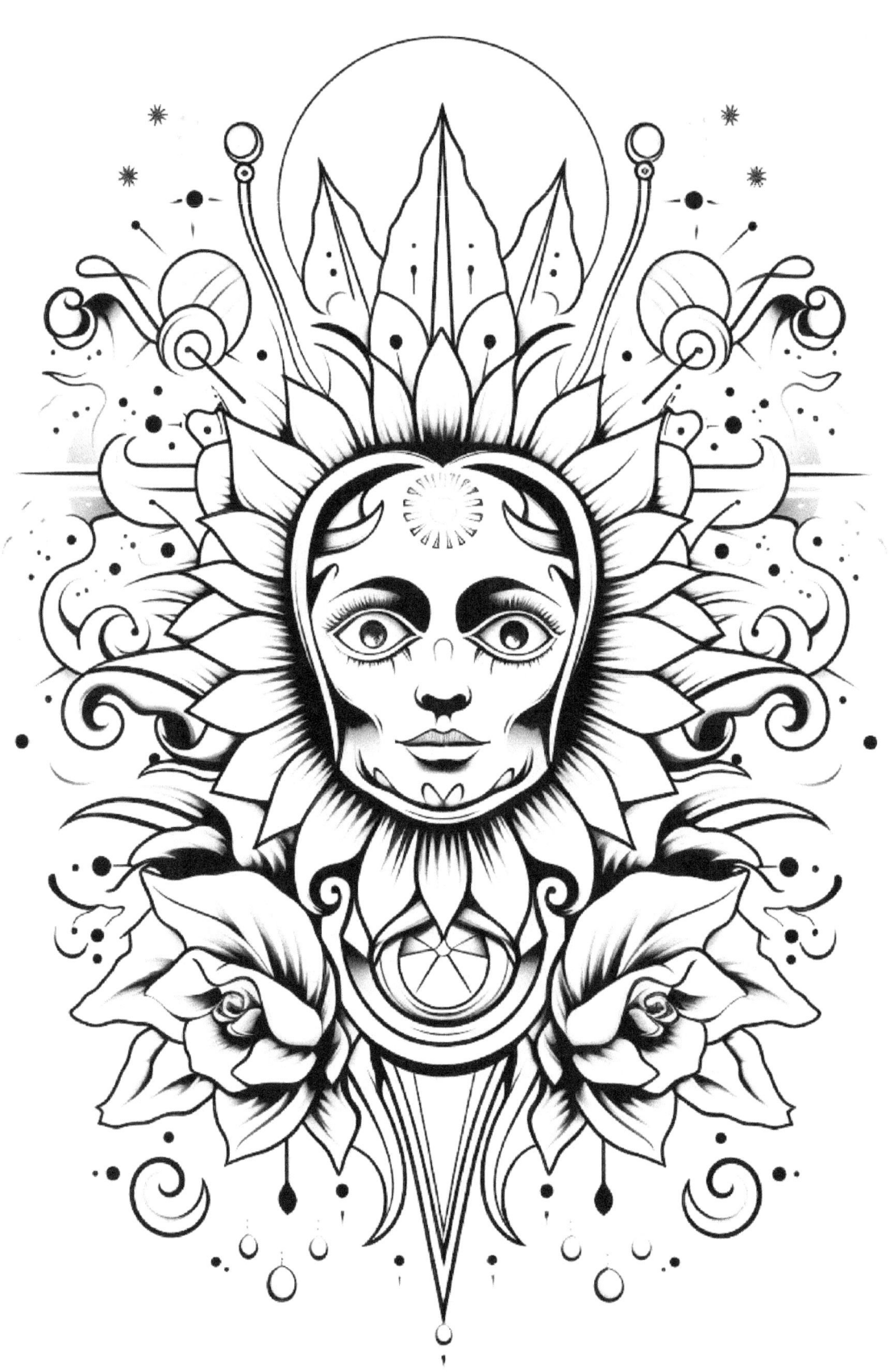

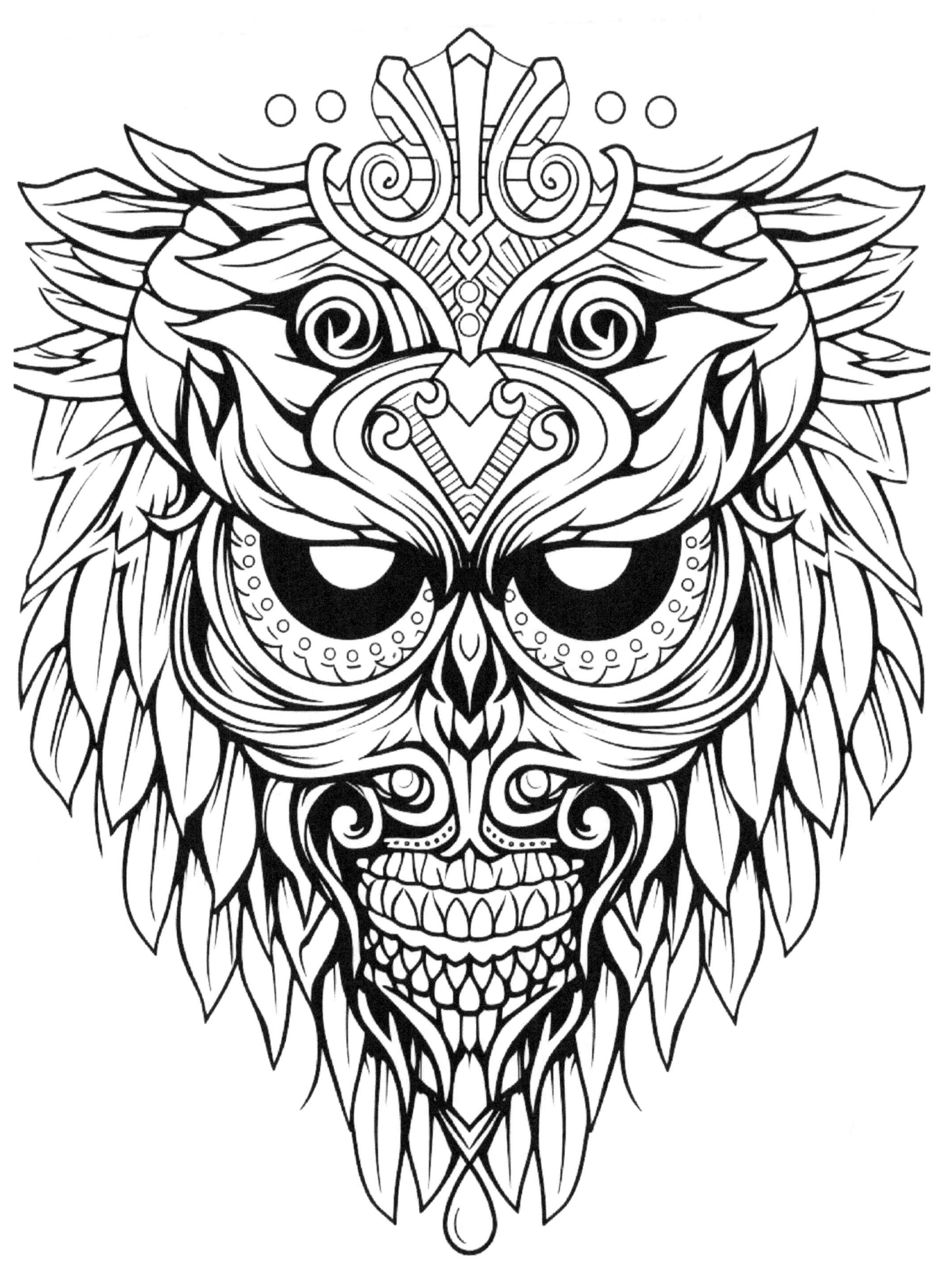

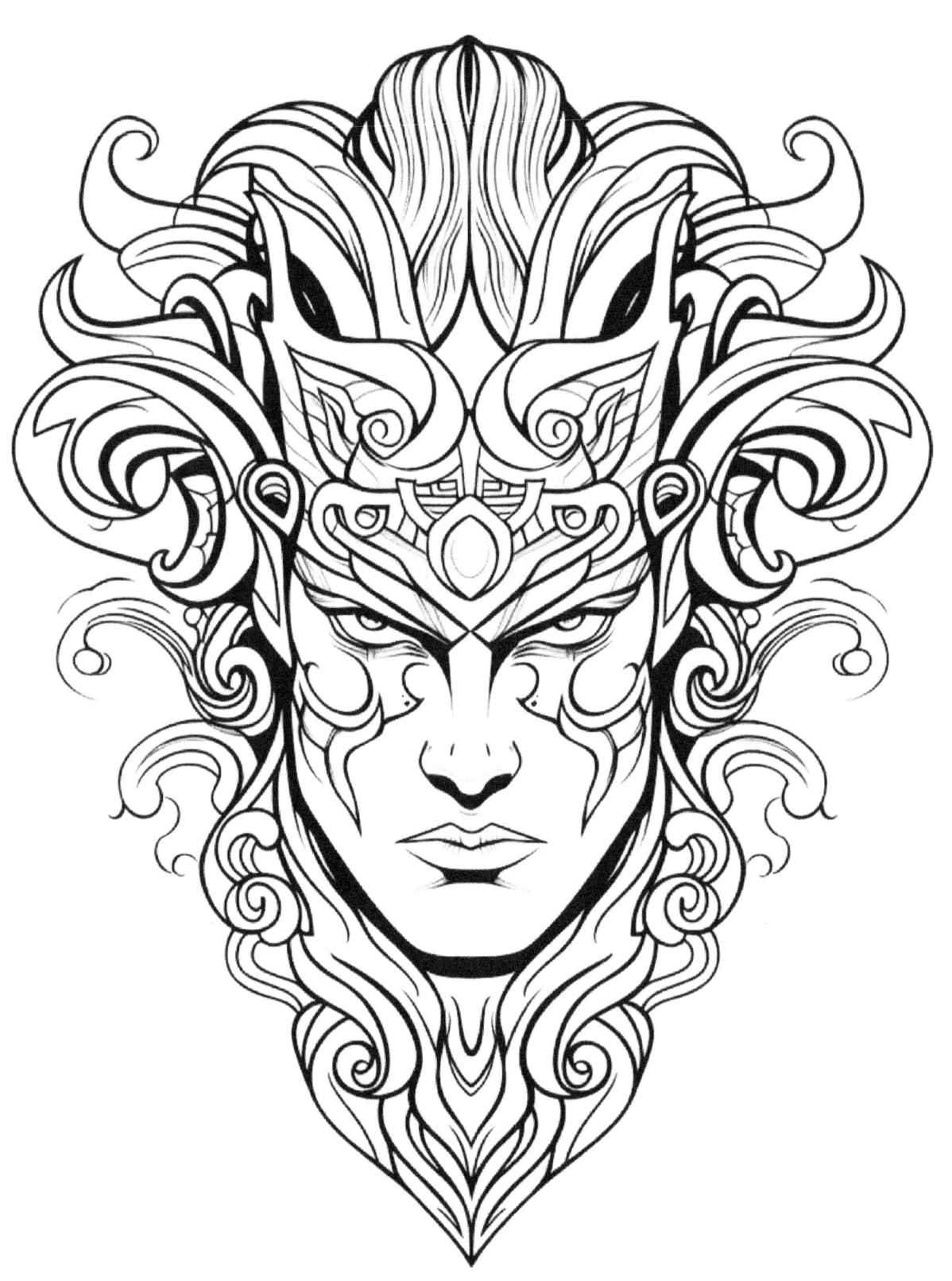

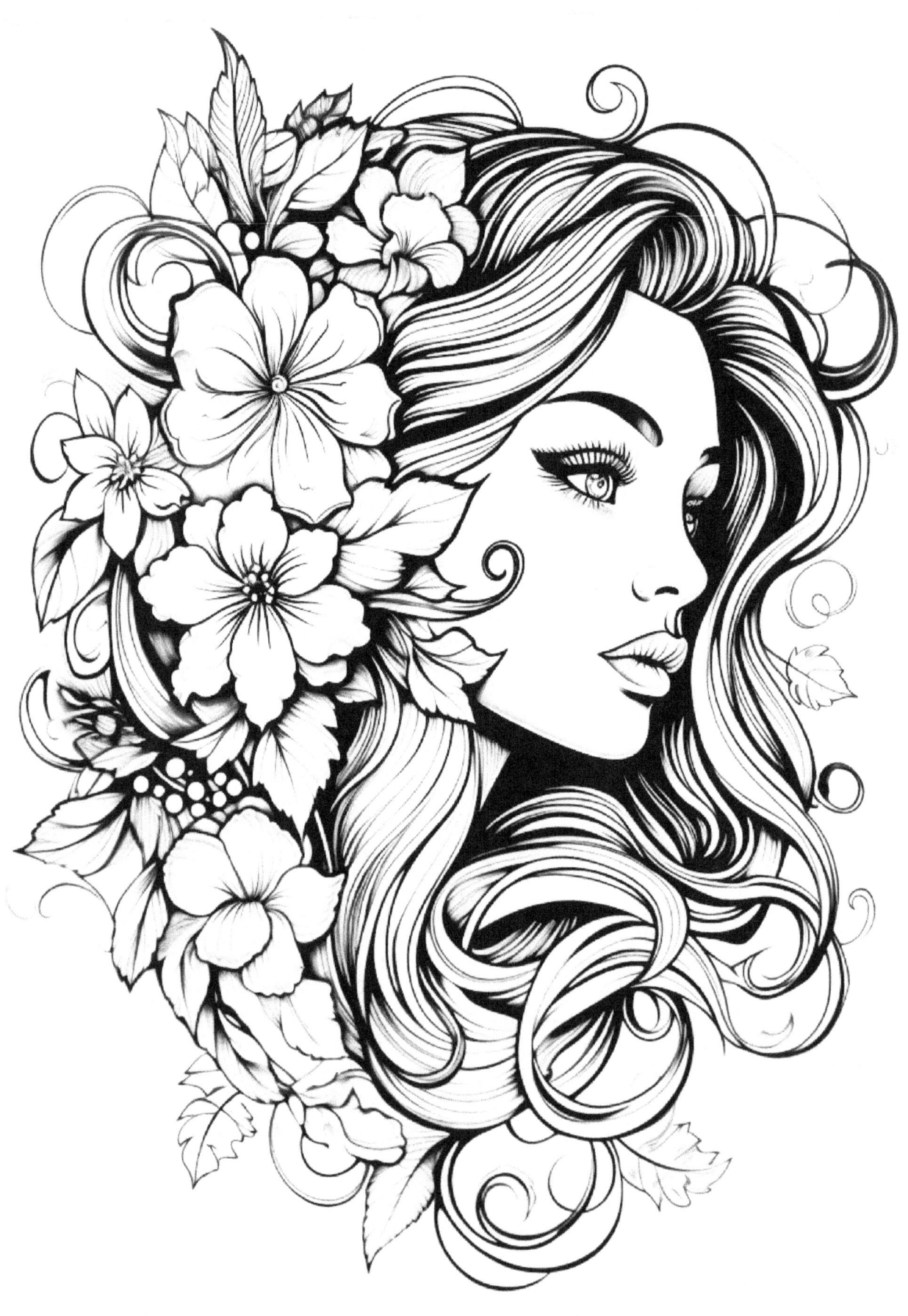

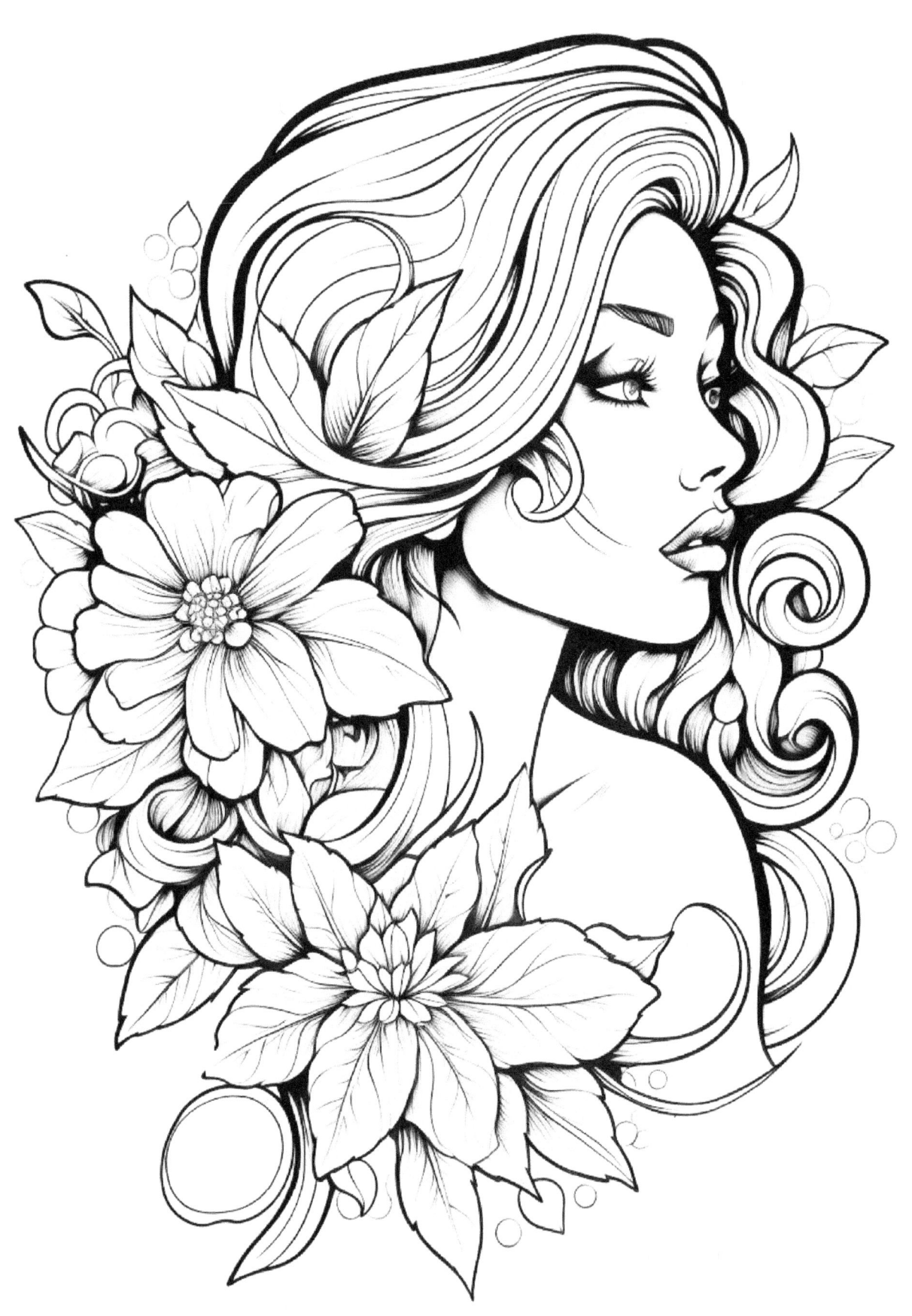